THE
COLLABORATION
ILLUSION

THE COLLABORATION ILLUSION

Why Working Together Sucks— and How to Fix It

ANCA CASTILLO & CARY LOPEZ, PHD

CURIOUS PEOPLE PRESS

The Collaboration Illusion: Why Working Together Sucks—and How to Fix It

First published in the USA in 2025 by Curious People Press, Phoenix, Arizona.

ISBN 979-8989767502 paperback
ISBN 979-8989767519 ebook

To anyone who has ever said,
"Collaboration shouldn't be this hard…"

We agree.

This book is for you.

CONTENTS

A Letter from the Authors 11
Tim's Story: Part 1 15

COLLABORATION SUCKS

A Brief History of Collaboration 21
Anca's story: Part 1—Falling for the Collaboration Illusion......... 30
The Collaboration Paradox: Where Social Pain and The
Collaboration Illusion Collide.. 36
Tim's Story: Part 2 39

THE SOCIETAL AND SYSTEMIC CHALLENGES OF COLLABORATION

Collaboration is Necessary (Future Perspective) 44
Cary's story: To meet or not to meet?... 50
So... What *Does* It Need to Be a Meeting? 51
   Recommendations: Want to Go Deeper on Meetings? 54
Tim's Story: Part 3... 55

SO, WHAT IS COLLABORATION?

From Projects to People to Pressure 62
Dimensions of Collaboration 63
The Quick Assessment 66
Our Story: Part 1—Low-Stakes Collaboration 69
Our Story: Part 2—High-Stakes Collaboration 71
The Need for Collaboration Process 73
The Positive Effects of High Stakes Collaboration Done Well....... 75
Anca's story: Part 2—The Faculty Meeting................................. 81
The Need for a Facilitator or Process Guide 83
Tim's Story: Part 4... 85
What is Visual Thinking Strategies (VTS)? 90

THE FACILITATOR AS PROCESS GUIDE

Tim's Story: Part 5.. 95

PRINCIPLES OF COLLABORATION

Foundational Principles of Great Collaboration 98
  Make the Abstract Clear 99
  Stop Assuming 103
  Just Say It 109
  Slow down to Speed Up 119
  Walk Away with Something Actionable...........................127
  Plan to Pivot 135
Tim's Story: Part 6..147

PUTTING IT INTO PRACTICE

From Learning to Leading...149
Tim's Story: Part 7..155

SUSTAINING LONG-TERM TEAM COLLABORATION

The Lifecycle of a Team..160
Tools to Help Teams Form 160
  Forming Activity 1: Guide to Me 162
  Forming Activity 2: Ways of Working 164
  Forming Activity 3: Values in Action 167
  Forming Activity 4: Planning for Conflict and Failure 173
  Forming Activity 5: Build Your Space Makers 176
  Forming Activity 6: Name Your Team 179
  Forming Activity 7: Craft a Team Charter/Mission 181
  Forming Activity 8: Map Your Team's Collaboration Rhythm ...184

NAVIGATING CONFLICT IN COLLABORATION

What Makes Conflict So Hard?...190
Conflict through the Principles of Collaboration 192
The Power of Perspective 202
How to Support a Team Through Conflict 208
A Call to Collaborate 211

RESOURCES

A Letter from the Authors

Over the past several years, we've been invited into rooms—real and virtual—where people are trying to do something together. Sometimes that "something" is strategic. Sometimes it's urgent. And sometimes, it's just messy and human.

As independent consultants (and before that, as in-house intrapreneurs in higher education), we've facilitated hundreds of sessions and worked with thousands of people, including faculty, staff, executives, students, government teams, nonprofit leaders, engineers, scientists, creatives.

No matter the project, the sector, or the personalities in the room, one thing remains true:

Collaboration is hard.

It doesn't matter how brilliant the individuals are or how noble the mission is, teams still get stuck. We see the same challenges surface again and again: unclear communication, decision-making gridlock, personality clashes, conflict avoidance (or explosion), broken trust, and the ever-present question of *how in the world do we move forward, together*?

Ironically, the more degrees, experience, or accolades someone has, the more difficult these collaborative basics can become. Intellect and experience can sometimes get in the way of connection.

After hearing, "Have you thought about writing a book?" for what felt like the umpteenth time, we put pen to paper.

This book is our attempt to distill the most useful, human, and field-tested insights we've learned about what makes collaboration work...and what gets in the way. We've written it for anyone who's ever left a meeting thinking, *there has to be a better way.*

Whether you're launching a new project, navigating a tough team dynamic, or just trying to get unstuck, our hope is that when you finish this book, you'll feel equipped, empowered, and prepared to engage in high-stakes collaboration. More than anything, we hope it helps you create interactions that are positive, productive, and maybe even inspiring.

Let's get to work.

—Anca & Cary

Meet Tim—The Collapse Before the Call

Standing at the front of the conference room, Tim wondered—for the third time that week—why on earth he had taken this job.

He could feel the tension in the air long before anyone said a word. On his left, the veteran engineers were bracing for another battle: arms folded, faces tight, eye contact avoidant. On his right, the newer team members looked restless and irritated by the team's inertia. Somewhere in the middle was Tim, hands in his pockets, mentally calculating how long he could stand there before someone exploded. Or walked out. Again.

Collaboration was part of his job. It said so right there in the job description. But no one warned him it would look like this. Like standing in a room where ten brilliant people couldn't agree on anything except how much they disliked working together.

Tim wasn't new to leadership. As the Director of Product Design at a large, respected organization, he knew how to run a team, deliver on deadlines, and push projects across the finish line. He loved seeing things launch. He loved impact. He loved pressure, even. He was good at his job.

But this part honestly just sucked. Collaboration.

He didn't like it. Didn't trust it. Didn't look forward to it. And if he was being honest, he kind of resented how often it showed up on his calendar.

The thing is, people liked Tim. He was personable, kind— the type of leader who remembered birthdays, brought cupcakes, and asked about your weekend. He cracked jokes. He showed up to potlucks. People thought he was an extrovert. But underneath it all, Tim was an introvert who preferred clarity over chaos, execution over discussion, and solo work over endless debate. When collaboration entered the room, joy exited.

And still, here he was.

He tried to refocus on the meeting in front of him. But instead, his mind drifted way back.

Before collaboration became a curse word in his world, there was a time when working with others was something he loved.

The Good Old Days (aka Baseball and Battle Bots)

Tim grew up with a baseball in his hand. His childhood was filled with dust, gloves, dugouts, and the unmistakable sound of a ball hitting a bat. His first team was Little League. His first coach? Coach Jefferson.

Coach Jefferson was like an egg: hard on the outside, soft on the inside. He was strict, no-nonsense, and the kind of man who could silence a team with a single look. He was also the first adult who ever told Tim it was okay to cry.

Tim had tried to slide into first base and rolled his ankle. He was eight years old and holding back tears with all the strength his body could muster. Coach Jefferson pulled him aside and said, "That was a brave move, Tim. I'm proud of you for trying. And hey, it's okay to cry. Don't ever be ashamed of having emotions. Especially when they mean something."

That moment stuck with Tim. So did the feeling of being part of a team. On the field, he knew what was expected of him. As a pitcher, he had a role, and he knew how his role fit into the bigger picture. Every player did. Drama? Handled by Coach. Confusion? Squashed with clarity. The team had structure, direction, and someone always leading the way.

When they won the championship that season, Coach Jefferson gathered the team, tears in his eyes, and said, "This happened because you worked together. You did your jobs. You showed up. You made it happen."

Tim never forgot that. He carried it with him into everything: Battle of the Books, student government, Habitat for Humanity, Battle Bots. He was the guy people wanted on their team: dependable, organized, enthusiastic. He loved the rhythm of a group working in sync.

But that all changed when the group Biology project happened.

The First Time Collaboration Sucked

It was freshman year of high school. Biology class. Mr. Roland was a rather grumpy older teacher who wore sweater vests and made way too many noises when he moved, like his body was protesting the idea of standing in front of unruly students and would rather be at home laying down on the couch. He stood at the front of the classroom with his usual clipboard and dry-erase marker and said, "Alright, your first project of the year will be a group collaboration project. You'll work in teams to build a model of a cell, with all of its parts, and present it to the class."

Tim blinked. Collaboration? It was the first time he'd heard the word.

He didn't raise his hand to ask what it meant; he didn't

want to look dense. So, he assumed it probably just meant teamwork. He was good at teamwork. He loved teamwork. He looked over at his friends and started imagining how they'd crush this project together. Then Mr. Roland continued: "I've already assigned your groups."

Tim's heart sank.

He was placed in a group with four classmates he barely knew. They dragged their backpacks over to a table and sat down awkwardly. Tim tried to stay upbeat. He smiled and broke the ice.

"So... what kind of cell do we want to do?"

Silence.

Five long seconds passed, although to Tim, it felt like five minutes. No one responded.

"...Okay," he said, filling the space. "How about a plant cell?"

No words. Just nods.

Tim took that as a yes. Perfect, he thought. Now we have a goal. Now we can do this.

He assumed the next step was obvious: divide and conquer. So, he asked, "What parts do you all want to take on?"

Again, nothing.

So, he started pointing.

"Can you bring the poster materials? Awesome! Can you make a list of the cell parts? Perfect! Would you like to write the descriptions? Okay. I can draw them. And you"—he pointed to the final (and unknown to him) quietest kid at the table— "you can do the final presentation."

More nods. Still no words.

It wasn't until later that Tim realized: he had never even introduced himself. He didn't know their names. He had stepped in, set the goal, handed out assignments, and started running the project, just like he always had during baseball or Battle Bots.

Only this time, it didn't work.

At their next group meeting in class, no one brought what they were supposed to. Everyone had forgotten.

Tim felt something he had never felt on a team before: alone.

He didn't know how to express his frustration. He didn't want to come off as mean. So instead, in a flat tone, he said, "That's fine. We'll just do it next week."

Next week came. Same result. Except this time, one kid had scribbled a quick list of cell parts on notebook paper. No one else had done anything. No one apologized. No one offered an explanation. They all just...sat there.

So, Tim did what he always did when something mattered: he took over.

He made the poster. He drew all the parts. He wrote the tiny labels. He memorized the script. He stood in front of the class and delivered the whole presentation like they'd all worked on it together.

They got an A.

And Tim hated every second of it.

I did all the work, he thought. *And they get the same grade? That is NOT fair! This sucks!*

Collaboration had left a bitter aftertaste that lingered long into adulthood.

After that, any time he heard the words "group project" or "collaboration," a part of him wanted to crawl under the table. He kept trying to recreate the structured, energized feel of his baseball team—but instead, he kept finding himself stuck in a dynamic where he did most of the work and everyone else got to coast.

And it didn't stop in high school. It followed him to college.

Then into meetings. Then boardrooms. Then every team-based project he ever led.

Collaboration, for Tim, had become a pattern he couldn't seem to break: one where he carried the weight, while others stood around, nodding along, saying nothing.

No wonder he hated it. He had never actually collaborated.

CHAPTER 1
Collaboration Sucks

"Alone we can do so little; together we can do so much."
–Helen Keller

The fact of the matter is: collaboration is hard. Some might even go as far as to say that collaboration sucks. Like Tim, we might find ourselves dreading the word along with the activities and actions that follow it. We know that we have to do it. There is no shortage of research, inspirational quotes, and stories that highlight the power of collaboration and how it can help us move faster, think bigger, and do more. However, no matter how much experience, knowledge, or accolades we have, we struggle with it.

You might be reading this and thinking to yourself, *I am a great collaborator. It is other people who suck at it and make collaborating hard and painful.* While that may be true for you, you might be surprised to know that while you are thinking this, others might be thinking the SAME thing at the same time about YOU. It is always easier to think that we are doing things right and "others" are doing things wrong.

But what if we are ALL doing it wrong at the same time?

A Brief History of Collaboration

From ancient tribal councils to modern-day boardrooms, collaboration (mostly in the form of conversation) has played a vital role in forming the social world as we know it today. Research in evolutionary biology has found that collaboration is one of the distinctive behaviors that separate humans from other mammals. In fact, scholars have proposed that "Human beings, and only human beings, are biologically adapted for participating in collaborative activities involving shared goals and socially coordinated action plans"[1]. If you think back to what would have originally driven us to collaborate, such as defending against fierce predators, building shelters, or finding food, these drivers may have been high stakes—after all, survival is pretty important—but they were *low complexity*. It's likely we still had to navigate interpersonal dynamics and relationships, but the driving goals of our efforts were shared and fairly easy to understand. We *had* to work together to survive.

Because it was so necessary, we likely didn't pay much attention to it. We never focused on what went right when it did go right, or what went wrong when it did go wrong. We just did it. It was thrust upon us with the expectation that we would just figure it out and do it...or else.

It wasn't until the early 20th century that we began to be aware of collective effort and to notice it as a "thing." That was when the Industrial Revolution brought about the first instances of large-scale, organized collaboration in factories and corporations[2]. It was then that we saw people who didn't know each other come together to do something that involved their communicating, combining ideas, finding solutions, playing off each other, and building a new path forward, all in a short span of time.

That is about the time when we began to truly feel the benefits of collaboration, along with how much it sucks when it does not go well. This is also about the time we as a species made a grave error and assumption, one that has cost us lots of time, effort, and emotional (and sometimes physical) pain.

Whether we like it or not, collaboration is all around us. Almost everything we interact with in our daily lives requires people to come together, to have conversations, and to work together toward a common purpose.

THE COLLABORATION ILLUSION
The assumption that because we are human and can communicate with each other, we must therefore naturally know how to collaborate.

Here's just a sampling of what we mean:

- Your coffee drink: *collaboration*
- The clothes and shoes you have on: *collaboration*
- The house or apartment you live in: *collaboration*
- The phone or car you are using: *collaboration*
- This book you are reading: *collaboration*
- Your computer: *collaboration*
- Your email software: *collaboration*
- The grocery store where you shop: *collaboration*
- The plane ride or hotel you have booked: *collaboration*
- The process of booking a plane or hotel: *collaboration*
- Conferences around the world you attend: *collaboration*
- Going to the moon: *collaboration*
- Tackling global climate change: *collaboration*

So, if collaboration is all around us, why is it so hard? Why do most people crinkle their noses and cross their arms at the idea of working in a group with other people? Shouldn't we have figured it out by now?

Your (Likely) Introduction to Collaboration (aka "Teamwork")

To better understand where our love/hate relationship with collaboration begins, we need to go back to our early childhood days. One of the first memories most of us have of collaboration (although it was not called *collaboration*) is through a familiar term many of us who grew up in the Western part of the world knew as "teamwork." As early as elementary school, most of us experience "teamwork" by engaging in sports, choir or band, drama or theater, some kind of after-school club, like student government or even Scouts. While the tasks in each of these activities may be different in nature, the make-up or structure of them all is essentially the same. First, they had an adult that was calling the shots. This adult was the leader, director, coach, or mentor of the group. They explained the rules, set the expectations, handled the conflicts and rewards, set the pace or rhythm of engagement, dealt with the consequences of loss or failure, dished out the punishment for non-performers, and they also handed out roles and responsibilities based on the skills and capabilities of each person.

In experiences like Tim's baseball team, this was the coach. The coach told you the rules of the game. They set the practice schedule. They evaluated the skills and capabilities of the players and assigned positions based on those evaluations. If you were messing around and not paying attention, they made you run extra laps. If you were under-performing, they pulled you from the action. If you were fighting with a teammate, they stepped in to mediate. Your role as a player was to stay in your lane, play to your strengths, follow the rules, be on time and focused, and be aware enough of the other players to be a good member of the team. If someone got hurt, you wanted to show compassion. If someone ran a great play, you made sure to congratulate them. If the entire team performed well and won a game, you got to celebrate in the shared accomplishment.

If you were part of a band, choir, drama, or theater group, like we were, the leader was the director. While on the surface it would be easy to think *but a band or dance troupe experience is entirely different from a sports team,* when you look at the structure of the collaboration itself, they are essentially the same. The director told you the rules of artistic engagement. They set the practice schedule. They evaluated the skills of the performers and assigned the chair, range, or role for which they would be best suited. If you were messing around and not paying attention, they made you sit out or start over again. If you were the star player, they awarded you the solo. If you had conflict with a band or cast member, they stepped in and mediated. Your role as a performer was to stay in your lane, play to your strengths, follow the rules, be on time and focused, and be aware enough of the other players to be a good member of the group. If someone needed support, you showed them compassion. If someone had a great performance or hit a great note, you congratulated them. If the entire ensemble performed well, everyone got to celebrate in the teamwork that allowed the performance to happen.

Are being in a band or musical group the same as being an athlete? No. But do the experiences from a *collaboration* standpoint seem eerily similar? Absolutely. Here's why: in these kinds of structured team activities, the guidelines for participation are very clear:

- There is a designated leader, who has the authority to punish and reward, as well as the knowledge about the activity to coach, guide, and mentor

- The roles of each member of the team are clearly articulated and well-known by everyone

- The goals and desired outcomes of the team's work together are familiar to everyone

- There is a set framework or structure for knowing what participation looks like (you show up, you practice, you perform, etc.)

- If anyone steps outside of their role, chaos will ensue

- The rules of the game/norms for behavior/expectations for performance are explicit, and the consequences for violating those rules are clear to everyone

- Successes are recognized and celebrated

- Failures are obvious and part of the learning process

- For most activities, there is a difference between practice and performance or "game time"

Now You

Pause for just a moment and reflect on your own experience with teamwork as you were growing up. Whether it was chess club, improv, dance, soccer, tennis or swim team, at first you had to consciously learn and understand the structured "rules of the game."

As you matured in your participation, those rules probably started to fade into the background a little bit, became part of "the common knowledge of how to be together" until one of the rules was violated, and then attention to the rules likely came back to the forefront for a while.

Now recall what "group work" or "collaboration" looked like in an academic context. Think back to elementary school. The idea of playing together with kids on a playground is fun and exciting. You make up games, rules, and allocated points, and the fun followed. As children, we are typically so excited to be around other children to just play.

Similarly, when your teacher said, "We are going to work in groups to build a book and present it," it was followed by clear instructions and pair or group assignments.

What happened? Typically, one of 2 things occurred:

1 As a group you began to argue about what the book should be, what the story was, who was writing what, who was presenting it to the class, who was drawing the pictures, etc., to the point where emotions were high and people began to shut down

Or

2 You quickly agreed on the book topic and who was doing what (which felt great) but as time went on, people had a hard time actually doing what had been agreed upon and animosity/fear crept in

In the end, similar to Tim's experience, the whole thing resulted into one or two people who took charge, made decisions, and gave orders/instructions while everyone else quieted and fell in line—all the while waiting for the project to be over. The story you began to tell yourself by the end of the experience was, *"Ughhh...I don't like group projects and would rather work by myself."*

And for most folks, this pattern probably continues into adulthood...

Most of us find ourselves in revolving roles: we are either one of those few people, like Tim, who take charge, make decisions, and tell everyone what to do, or we are the quiet followers, like Tim's group members, who are there for the awkward and unpleasant ride.

For most of us, this unpleasant experience of collaboration leaves such a bad taste in our mouth that even before "collaboration" has the chance to be positive and productive, it is doomed because we expect it to be doomed. We walked in dreading it, with a history of baggage and bad experiences, assuming the worst, expecting chaos, trying to avoid conflict, and waiting for the sweet moment when it is over. If any of the "bad" that we assume will happen does in fact happen, we say, "Yup, that is why collaboration sucks!" It is a self-perpetuating loop of doom.

But the honest truth is, it is not our fault!

It is not our fault if we are one of the few people who take the lead because things are not moving forward. Someone has to or else nothing would happen, and we would fail.

And it is not our fault if we are one of the people that become quiet, fall in line, and are along for the ride because at some point, someone has to give in to the bigger, louder voices or else it would just be shouting and arguing all the time. And there is only so much of that any of us can take.

 **So if it is not our fault, whose fault is it?**
Meet the *Collaboration Illusion.*

This is the fault of the *Collaboration Illusion.* The *Collaboration Illusion* tells us that because we are human and can communicate with each other, we must therefore naturally know how to collaborate. That is probably why Tim's teacher Mr. Roland just threw everyone in his freshman biology class into groups and asked them to collaborate on the cell project without any other instructions, guide, best practices, mentoring, mediation, or support. We would wager to guess that Mr. Roland himself had a very similar experience growing up as well, which is why he did the same thing for this class. And why not? The kids figured it out; it's a sink or swim situation. You either do it, or you don't. There's a presentation at the end, or there isn't. And for most of us, we figured out a way to do it, like Tim and his group did.

But did they enjoy it? **NO.**

Was it a positive and productive experience? **NOPE!**

The *Collaboration Illusion* has prevented us from thoroughly examining what dynamics foster good collaboration. Not only this, but within the Illusion is hidden another belief: that the smarter we are (the more schooling, experience, and accolades we have), the better we should be at collaborating. So, not only do we assume that because we can communicate, we can collaborate, but we also assume that the smarter and more accomplished we are, the more equipped we are at collaboration. From our experience, these assumptions are wrong.

ANCA'S STORY: PART 1—FALLING FOR THE COLLABORATION ILLUSION

I admit that I have fallen victim to this part of the *Collaboration Illusion.* When I was an associate director at a large research university, I found myself surrounded by some of the best and brightest scholars in the country, who were advancing incredible and innovative research. I saw the faculty as being brilliant and capable and really admired them. So, you can imagine my excitement when an associate dean invited me to be a fly on the wall to a meeting where 15 faculty members were coming together to collaborate on a new interdisciplinary graduate degree. This degree program was pioneering, the first of its kind, and would require integrating multiple disciplines that, despite their similarities, had historically operated independently and never collaborated across their established boundaries.

I was excited to see what this collaborative conversation would sound like, what this process would look like, what this brilliant exchange of ideas and energy would feel like. Then, 10 minutes into the Zoom call, I was in shock. These 15 outstanding individuals did not engage in a collaborative exchange of ideas; instead, they were name calling, belittling, bashing, and outright being rude to each other. It was a good thing my camera was off so that no one could see the face I made when one faculty bluntly said to another, "No one cares about your class."

They could not agree on anything. They each were convinced that their class was the best class and thus should be a core class of this interdisciplinary degree, and they were battling it out as if they had on boxing gloves. The associate dean who brought them together had no idea what to do. While intelligent, he was not comfortable with conflict and was in way over his head at this point.

I left that 60-minute meeting stunned, thinking, How is it that some of the keenest minds in our country cannot come together to collaborate on this? How have we come to fail them in this way? How is it that they don't know how to do it?

I didn't know it at the time, but I had fallen victim to the *Collaboration Illusion*: I had assumed that because they were brilliant leaders in their field, with PhDs and lots of experience, that they would know how to collaborate. That they SHOULD know how to collaborate. Oh, how wrong I was.

As opposed to the structured experiences like team sports or music, the "rules" of collaboration seem to be entirely different, or even, non-existent:

- There *may* be a leader, director, coach, or mentor who understands the "rules of the game" and has the authority to enforce those rules and reward good performance...or not

- There *may* be a clear or stated outcome or goal...or not

- Each member *may* understand their specific role, and both their own strengths and the strengths of the other members of the group...or not

- There *may* be clearly articulated rules or behavioral norms the group has agreed to abide by...or not

- There *may* be opportunities to practice or try things and learn from failure...or not

- There *may* be a clear understanding of what is expected of you in participating in the group exercise...or not

With all of the ambiguity around what "good" collaboration looks like, it's no wonder we cringe when we're asked to work with others. And in the absence of not knowing how to collaborate or what good collaboration requires, we do what we normally do: we substitute our lack of knowledge with an experience that is close to what we're currently in, and hope for the best.

TIM'S STORY: A MISTAKE IN THE MAKING

When Tim walked into the next meeting with the engineering team, he had a plan.

He was done watching people talk in circles. Done with the endless bickering. Done trying to get consensus through sheer patience.

He was going to treat the team like his baseball team: simple, structured, and goal-oriented.

It had worked before—after all, his little league team had won the championship. So why wouldn't the same principles work now?

He walked into the room channeling full Coach Jefferson energy. He'd be the egg: hard on the outside, soft on the inside. He'd set the goal. He'd name the roles. He'd lead them across the finish line in three months, just like Coach would have.

He even smiled as he walked in.

The team sat around the table, laptops open, arms crossed, coffee half-drunk and cooling beside them. They weren't a team yet. They were two groups of strangers sharing a project they didn't agree on. Five veterans, emotionally tied to the existing product. Five new engineers, hungry to innovate. And Tim, somewhere in the middle, tried to herd cats with a Gantt chart.

"Alright," he said, standing confidently at the front of the room, hands crossed over his chest. "You're all brilliant. You're all critical to this project. And we have three months left to make this redesign happen. So we're going to scrap the old design entirely and build something brand new."

Silence.

The veterans (i.e., the engineers who had poured years of work into the original product) shifted in their seats. Some uncrossed and re-crossed their arms. Some glanced at each other with narrowed eyes. One of them, Sam, inhaled sharply through his teeth. Tim didn't catch it.

Meanwhile, the newbies leaned in. Tim could practically see the energy buzz through them. Finally, someone had said the thing they were hoping to hear. They were excited. A direction! A decision! And one they agreed with.

But Tim, in his inner monologue, was already onto the next bullet point. Step one: set the vision. Check.

Now: assign roles.

He hesitated. He didn't know the team well enough to confidently assign tasks based on strengths. So, he figured a middle-ground approach would do.

"Who wants to start figuring out the updated needs of our customers and translate them into a design blueprint?"

Crickets.

"Okay... who wants to take the design blueprint and build a prototype?"

All five newbies raised their hands like eager students.

Before Tim could say more, Jessica, a veteran member of the team who had helped design the original product, raised her hand.

"Sorry, but I don't agree," she said, voice calm but sharp. "I don't understand why we have to scrap the old design. It's one of our key differentiators. Sure, we've been losing a few customers, but that doesn't mean we throw away the whole thing."

The other veterans murmured in agreement. You could feel the shift in the room: the lines being drawn.

Marcus, one of the newer engineers, jumped in. "Actually,

I do think we need to scrap it. We need to stay competitive. That means starting from scratch. The old design was great... ten years ago. Now it's just outdated."

Tim could feel the tension rising, but he was committed to his Coach Jefferson role. "Listen," he said, trying to sound both firm and motivational. "We're a team. And like any team, we need to pull together, focus on our goal, and play our roles. We don't have time to debate this endlessly."

Jessica's face flushed red. "This isn't some sports game, Tim! You're dismissing years of work."

Trying to salvage control, Tim clapped his hands once. "Alright! Let's not lose focus. Marcus—you and the new engineers take charge of the prototype. Jessica—you and the veterans can ensure the new design incorporates anything essential from the old one."

The veterans looked at one another with disbelief.

Jessica pushed her chair back. "This isn't working. You're not listening to us. You're just dictating. That's not collaboration."

Sam, another veteran added, "What we need is trust. And right now, we don't feel any."

Tim raised his voice, panic tightening in his chest. "We're wasting time! I need everyone to step up and do their part."

It was the final crack.

Jessica gathered her things. "I can't work like this."

One by one, the veteran engineers stood and followed her out of the room. The door closed behind them with a sharp *click*.

Tim stood there, stunned. The newer engineers looked equally frozen. No one spoke.

His plan, his big "Coach Jefferson" moment, had blown up spectacularly.

Well-intentioned? Sure. Effective? Not even close.

Tim stared down at the table. His stomach twisted. His confidence had crumbled.

This wasn't something he could fix with a pep talk and a plan.

The Collaboration Paradox: Where Social Pain and The Collaboration Illusion Collide

If dealing with the *Collaboration Illusion* wasn't enough, there is another contributing factor that prevents us from naturally being good collaborators: social pain.

Social pain is defined as "...the process by which rejection and exclusion recruits similar neural circuits as physical pain, generating an effectual response that mirrors the response one feels from physical trauma". In other words, when we experience social rejection, or even *fear* that if we do or say something wrong we will no longer belong to a group, we neurologically experience the same kind of emotional response as we would if we were physically injured.

Let that sit for a moment.

Our brain experiences *social pain* the same way it experiences *physical pain*.

Tim and his team of engineers just experienced social pain. The engineers who created the original software feel dismissed and undervalued; the newer engineers feel bewildered and like their opinion is meaningless. Now there are factions within the group, i.e., the "old guard" vs. the "new guard," and no one feels they belong with the group as a whole.

Combine this concept of *social pain* with what we've learned about our basic, biological need to collaborate. These are two opposing forces: on the one hand, our survival instinct tells us we must work together to survive and thrive; on the other hand, working with others means potentially being vulnerable to social pain, which we also biologically avoid at all costs.

Thus, the Collaboration Paradox emerges: we must collaborate, and in doing so, we must embrace the possibility of being hurt by the people we are collaborating with.

The Collaboration Paradox
The tension we feel between these 2 opposing forces

If you are reading this book, it is probably because you have felt the pain of bad collaboration in your own life. You have seen how horrible and defeating it feels to try to work with a group of people on something meaningful and to have it not go well, despite your best efforts and intentions. By now, hopefully you feel that you are not alone in that feeling, and you understand the *Collaboration Illusion* and Collaboration Paradox are to blame.

No wonder so many of us struggle with it. No wonder Tim hates it. But the struggle with collaboration is more than just a personal thing. It is a societal and systemic challenge as well.

The Call For Help

Tim sat in his car for a long time after that meeting. The sun was low, casting the amber end-of-day light that made the dashboard glow. He wasn't ready to go home just yet. He knew his wife, Allison, would be there, probably making dinner, probably waiting to ask how the day went. He didn't have it in him to pretend it was fine.

Eventually, he pulled into the driveway, stepped inside, and dropped his bag by the door with a thud. Allison turned from the kitchen with a gentle, knowing smile.

"How was it?" She asked.

Tim paused. "Well... I tried something new."

"Oh no," she said, already bracing.

"I went full Coach Jefferson."

She burst out laughing. "Oh no."

"Oh yes," Tim groaned, rubbing his face. "I stood up, made a big speech about goals and teams and roles...and within thirty minutes, half the room walked out. Literally walked out."

Allison tried to contain her laughter. "You've always had a Coach Jefferson story for every leadership challenge you've ever faced. I was wondering when that one was going to show up at work."

Tim chuckled, but it was hollow. "I don't know what to do. I honestly don't. I've never felt this stuck."

Allison paused, then said gently, "You know, maybe it's time to talk to someone who actually knows how to fix this. Someone whose whole job is around helping teams of people collaborate better. I have a couple of friends who might be able to help."

Tim didn't respond right away. He hated asking for help. Not out of pride, just out of habit. But this time was different. Something about having people walk out shook something loose in him.

After dinner, he sat at the kitchen table, opened his laptop, and typed an email.

Need Support with Collaboration

Hi Cary and Anca,

My name is Tim. I'm currently leading a product redesign team that's struggling to make progress. The project is high-stakes, the team dynamics are rough, and despite my best efforts, things are falling apart.

My wife Allison mentioned your work, and I'd love to see if there's a chance you can help us get back on track.

Thanks for considering,
Tim

We met Tim two days later on a Zoom call. He looked tired. Not the overworked kind of tired, but the *I'm carrying too much and don't know where to put it down* kind of tired.

After introductions and a bit of small talk, we asked him the same discovery questions we ask all our clients. The ones designed to surface both the big picture and the messy human parts underneath.

He told us about the project:

"It's a redesign of our flagship product. Sales are slipping, and leadership wants a bold solution."

He told us about the team:

"There are ten engineers. Five veterans who built the original product. Five newer folks who want to start from scratch."

He told us about the culture:

"There's tension. They don't trust each other. They don't talk. Or when they do, it's just arguing."

He told us about his approach :

"I tried everything I knew how to do. And I made it worse."

Then he said the words we hear more often than people expect:

"I don't know what to do. I'm at my wit's end. But I really, really want this to work."

We sat with that for a moment.

Then we told him the truth.

"Tim, you're not alone. This is exactly when most people reach out to us: after they've already tried everything they know how to do and nothing's working. The good news? This is fixable. The tricky part? It's not going to be fast. It's going to require slowing down, doing things that don't always make logical sense at first, and addressing some human stuff that's been pushed aside. But we can help you build something that actually lasts. Are you willing to trust the process?"

Tim exhaled. You could see it: the shift. Not relief exactly, but something close to it. Like someone had finally said, *"You're not crazy. This is hard. And also, there's a way through."*

He nodded.

"Yes," he said. "Let's do it."

CHAPTER 2
The Societal and Systemic Challenges of Collaboration

Even though we know that collaboration and collaborative conversations are key to developing innovative ideas, strategies, products, and businesses, and despite the large amounts of studies and books about collaboration, people still struggle with it. The rise of remote work, diverse workforces, and rapid technological changes only adds to the complexity of collaborative efforts.

At this point, you might be reading this and thinking to yourself, "You are blowing this out of proportion and making it a bigger problem than it actually is."

You might be surprised to learn that as of 2023, approximately 70% of projects fail to deliver their intended outcomes, often due to issues rooted in ineffective collaboration and communication[3]. These collaboration struggles don't just affect people: they have tangible impacts on budgets, timelines, and overall success. For instance, projects that lack effective collaboration tools or processes often experience budget overruns and delays, sometimes by as much as 30 to 45%[4],[5]. Moreover, organizations that undervalue soft skills like communication and teamwork lose 47% more of their budgets due to project failure compared to those that prioritize these skills.[6]

So, when leaders ask, "Why does collaboration matter so much?" it's because collaboration isn't just a "soft skill."

Collaboration is a critical success factor. And when it goes wrong, everything else can unravel.

More than that, it is not just the time, money, and success of the project that are impacted by poor collaboration. If unhealthy collaboration persists, it can impact people's hope, trust, job satisfaction, morale, mental health, and physical health.

Collaboration is not only important because of the work. It is important because of its unseen impacts on the people doing the work.

Collaboration is Necessary (Future Perspective)

The need to collaborate and engage in collaborative conversations is not going anywhere. If anything, it will be more important and more critical with trends like globalization, the gig economy, and even artificial intelligence (AI).

The challenges of tomorrow are bigger, more complex, and more integrated than ever before. As such, they will require more and more people to come together to use our collective wisdom to collaborate, and to engage in collaborative conversations where every voice is heard, every possibility is explored, and everyone works together to move things forward.

With the introduction of AI and machine learning, people fear that their jobs or roles might become obsolete. While this may be a reality for jobs based on administrative tasks, data analysis and reporting, or other tasks machine learning and AI can do better and faster than humans, these technologies lack the nuanced understanding and emotional intelligence required for truly effective collaboration.

For example, while AI can help us research and synthesize all the possible solutions for single-use plastic, it cannot promote cross-industry collaboration that brings together leaders, makes them feel comfortable, invites them to share best practices, and encourages them to find a new path forward to change consumer behavior. Only people can do that, and only those versed and skilled in the art of collaboration can do that *well*.

 **So we ask again...why is collaboration so hard?**

Aside from the reasons we've touched on, (like the fact that most of us were never taught *how* to collaborate but were still expected to be good at it), there are some deeper, messier truths.

We call these the **human factors**. Things like:

- social loafing (when someone lets others do the heavy lifting, but still gets credit)[7]
- fear of confrontation
- resistance to change
- personality differences
- communication styles or language barriers
- cultural misunderstandings
- hidden assumptions or unconscious biases
- lack of trust or connection
- power dynamics

And then, there are logistical barriers:

- time zones
- tech platform overload
- business jargon and acronyms that feel like a foreign language

In short, the odds are not in our favor when it comes to collaboration.

Yet, we keep trying to fix collaboration with more stuff, and specifically, with more technology.

A 2023 study by Microsoft found that employees spend on average 57% of their time using technology just to communicate[8]. Between communication channels like Slack and Microsoft Teams, project platforms like Asana and Monday.com, and integrated systems like Salesforce and Google Workspace, we are surrounded by more ways to "collaborate" than ever before.

But here's the thing: collaboration isn't a tool problem, it's a *people* problem. Throwing more apps at it isn't going to solve the real issue.

And don't even get us started on meetings (aka, "where hope goes to die").

One study found that 37% of a worker's week is spent planning for, or sitting in, meetings[9]. As we saw with Tim and his team, more meetings rarely mean better collaboration. If anything, they often become another symptom of the dysfunction.

Part of the problem goes back to the *Collaboration Illusion*: the idea that because people are talking to each other, they must be collaborating. Because meetings involve talking, we've conflated *meetings* with *collaboration*.

Whether it's Zoom, Teams, or a huddle in the conference room, meetings have become the de facto solution for "doing work together." But are they actually helping?

Before we dive into what good collaboration *does* look like, we need to unpack how it often shows up in organizations, which is primarily through meetings and information exchange.

Let's start with the basics: why do we even gather people in the first place? It usually comes down to two core needs:

 ## *Information + Knowledge Sharing*

At a functional level, people come together to exchange information. But information and its forms--what we need to do with it, and how we use it—are not all the same.

For example, are we simply needing an update on something? Or does our team need to actively work with another team to accomplish something together that neither team can do alone?

To understand how and when to collaborate, we first need to better understand the types of information we need from one another:

TYPE	DESCRIPTION	NEEDS
Information sharing	Status updates, decisions, timelines, roles	The "who needs to know what" basics. Minimal interaction required.
Knowledge sharing	Clarifying something, offering advice, debating a topic to reach a shared understanding.	Some interaction, some interpretation.
Co-creation	Actively working together to make something—like a document, strategy, or plan.	Collaborative creation. *Requires* mutual input and ownership.
Problem-solving / Decision-making	Arguably the most intense form of collaboration—because you need more than information.	You need other people's brains, creativity, and perspectives to make progress.

2   *Belonging + Connection*

As we've stated, it's not just about the work. Remember, as humans we have a biological need to connect with others[10]. And that plays out in our work lives too. When people feel like they belong, *everything* gets better. A 2019 *Harvard Business Review* study showed that high belonging was linked to:

- a 56% increase in job performance
- a 50% drop in turnover risk
- a 75% reduction in sick days[11]

If you're a manager or team lead, and you're trying to help people feel like they matter, what's the obvious move?

Maybe you bring them together. Maybe you schedule a meeting. But that's how we got *here*.

We're not saying that meetings are inherently bad. They're not. People need time to connect, build trust, and work through ideas together. But when meetings become the *only* way we think collaboration happens, we've lost the plot.

And it's not making sense . A 2022 survey found that 69% of employees feel lonely at work, despite being in more meetings than ever before[12]. This should tell us something.

More meetings ≠ better collaboration.
More tools ≠ better connection.

If anything, these efforts often make the problem worse. Before we can start designing better collaboration, we have to *unmix* the mess we're in.

This means asking:

- What are we really trying to do together?
- What kind of exchange does it require?
- And what kind of space or format will actually help us do it?

Let's start here.

CARY'S STORY: TO MEET OR NOT TO MEET?

It was Sunday night. I was lying in bed, staring at my calendar and trying to mentally prepare myself to tackle the week. My phone screen glowed with the grim reality: almost every day was booked with back-to-back meetings. A few were in person. Most were virtual. All of them felt... heavy.

Among all those back-to-back meetings, I had a massive deadline to hit by Friday, and it was a project that required deep focus, creative thinking, and uninterrupted time.

Spoiler alert: that time did not exist on my calendar.

I felt my stomach sink. "Guess it's going to be another 60-plus hour week," I muttered to myself. I was used to working late nights to get my "real work" done. But this week? That wasn't even an option, because it was concert week at my kids' schools. Choir performances. Instrument showcases. Evening events I wanted and needed to be at.

That's when the realization hit me: I was going to have to decline some meetings.

The thought alone made my chest tighten. As a recovering people-pleaser, I hate letting people down. Saying no, even to a meeting, feels like telling someone their dog is ugly.

Out of desperation, I scanned the meeting titles and agendas (or, at least the ones that had agendas):

- Project Alpha Status Update
- Team Check-In
- Presentation of Findings
- 1:1 Catch-up
- Quick Touch-Base on Project Zede

Huh.

It hit me like a lightning bolt: *most of these meetings were just information dumps*. They weren't collaborative. They weren't strategic. They weren't creative. Nope, they were all updates. Almost all of them could be replaced by an email, a shared doc, or a Slack message.

Only the ones involving one-on-one meetings with teammates, sensitive dynamics, or relationship-building felt like they truly needed to happen in real time.

Then came the questions I had somehow never seriously asked myself: *Why had I never looked critically at my calendar before?*

Were all these meetings really necessary?

The answer was probably *no*. But if I wanted to start saying "no" more often, I needed a better framework for deciding what actually *needed* to be a meeting, and what didn't.

So... What *Does* It Need to Be a Meeting?

Let's break it down.

When deciding whether something *needs* to be a meeting, ask yourself:

1. **What's the purpose of the interaction?**
   Are you sharing information? Making a decision? Creating something together? Just checking in?

2. **Do you need other people to get it done?**
   Is this a solo update or a group solve?

3. **Will this interaction help strengthen a relationship?**
   In a world where loneliness and disconnection are on the rise, this one matters more than most of us realize.

Once you know what type of communication you're dealing with, and what your relational goals are, you can match it to the right interaction format. Here's a simplified matrix we often use:

PURPOSE	RELATIONAL IMPACT	DEPENDENCY ON OTHERS	BEST FORMAT
Sharing info or status updates	Low	Low	Email, Slack, shared doc, dashboard
Answering questions / clarifying information	Low	Low-Medium	Email, Slack, 1:1, Project Management Software (Asana, Wrike, Monday, Trello), or other digital tools
Co-creating something	Medium	High	Shared Google Doc / OneDrive document, an editing meeting, collaborative whiteboards, other digital tols
Problem-Solving or Decision-Making	High	High	Meeting, workshop, retreat, design sprint

Of course, not every decision is this clean. For Cary, canceling half her meetings that week gave her short-term breathing room; but meetings like project updates and weekly stand-ups are part of the rhythm of work. You can't just cancel them all and hope things magically stay aligned.

This framework helps you evaluate *individual* interactions, but not the longer arc of *organizational meeting culture*. And that culture matters.

Our colleague Elise Keith at Lucid Meetings developed a typology of 16 unique types of meetings, each with different collaborative, informational, and relational implications[13]. Add in the social norms and unspoken expectations that come with *how* meetings are done at your organization, and it's no wonder most of us feel like we're drowning in calendar invites.

This book isn't about fixing your meeting culture (though we'll offer some tools that can help). We're sharing this story, and the framework above, to make one simple point:

We've mistaken meetings for collaboration.

But they're not the same thing.

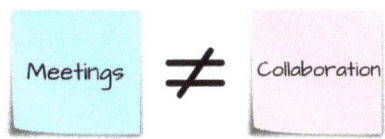

Meetings are a ***container***. Collaboration is what may—or may not—happen inside these meetings.

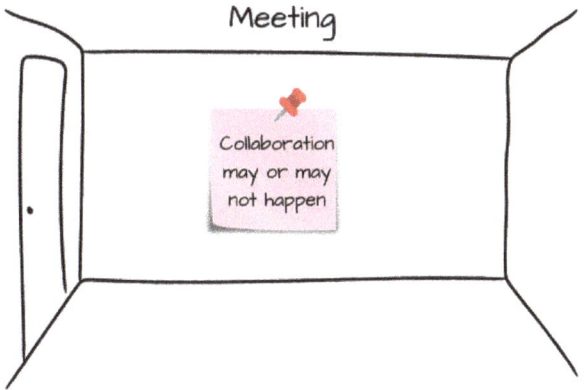

It's time to dig into **what collaboration actually is.** It is time to see how we were able to help Tim and his team.

Recommendations: Want to Go Deeper on Meetings?

If you're someone who wants to get serious about transforming your meetings, we've got you. There's an entire field of experts who focus on exactly this:

Meeting experts:
- Elise Keith, Lucid Meetings (lucidmeetings.com)
- Dr. Carrie Goucher, FewerFasterBolder (fewerfasterbolder. com)
- Lee Gimpel, Better Meetings (bettermeetings.expert)

Communities of practice:
- Meeting Professionals International (mpi.org)
- The Meeting Innovation Community (meetinginnovation. community)

Playful spaces for experimentation:
- New Rules for Work (newrulesforwork.com)

Want the Research?

Check out *The Cambridge Handbook of Meeting Science* (Allen, Lehmann-Willenbrock, & Rogelberg).

Prefer tech tools?
Try exploring AI-powered meeting assistants and productivity platforms. (Search "AI productivity tools for meetings" and dive in.) Now that we've looked at what collaboration is *not*:

- It's not teamwork the way we learned it in high school
- It's not the group project where one person does everything
- It's not meetings

Chapter 2 Done!

A Team Divided

Tim wasn't sure what to expect when bringing the team back together.

He had gratefully, and a little nervously, asked to bring us in. The memory of the last meeting still lingered like a bad smell. People stormed out. Raised voices. A silence so sharp it could slice through a whiteboard. The last thing he wanted was a repeat scenario.

He also knew he couldn't fix this alone.

When the day came for the first facilitated session with us, Tim arrived early. The conference room was quiet, almost too quiet, like it knew what was coming. Tim checked the markers. Adjusted the chairs. Opened the windows for some air. Then he waited.

One by one, the engineers filed in. The veterans came together, silent and tight-lipped, settling into the same side of the room. The newbies clustered on the other end, chatting softly. It was like watching a middle school dance: two groups, one room, a whole lot of distance.

Tim gave a tight smile. Then we stepped in, greeted the group, and began.

" We're here to support this team in doing one of the

hardest things any team can do, which is collaborate under pressure. Before we jump into anything, we want to start with some ground rules."

A large poster on the wall read:

- Listen to understand, not to judge.
- Assume positive intent.
- Be vulnerable—say the thing, even when it's hard.
- Don't use abbreviations—clarity helps everyone.
- Stay engaged.
- Trust the process.

Tim watched as people nodded along, some skeptically, some curiously.

Then came the first exercise.

"We want to start by reconnecting as humans," Anca said. "So, we have a simple question: What is one ordinary moment in your daily life that brings you pure joy?"

People blinked.

"We know, it's a little different," Cary added. "But give it a try. Write it down on a sticky note, and then we'll go around and introduce ourselves: your name, role, and your moment of joy."

Tim panicked for a moment. Joy? He couldn't even remember the last time he thought about that. But he scribbled something down anyway: *Scaring my wife and adding it to our prank compilation video.*

As the group shared, something started to shift. Jessica talked about walking her dog each morning. Marcus chimed in that he walks his dog every evening. They laughed—a small but meaningful connection. Tim's story made the whole room laugh—no one had pictured him as the prankster type.

It wasn't magic. But it was something.

Scaring my wife and adding it to our prank compilation video.

The next exercise dug a little deeper and started to get the group talking about the dreaded product redesign. They were invited to do a **Rose, Thorn, Bud** activity:

 Rose (pink): What do you love about the existing product? What has worked well? What impact has it made?

 Thorn (blue): What's not working? What's outdated or causing issues?

 **Bud** (green): What are the opportunities? The ideas or possibilities you're curious about?

Cary and Anca distributed sticky notes to each person and asked them to reflect and write quietly for a few minutes. Then, the team took turns reading and posting their thoughts.

The wall filled quickly.

Then it happened: a shift in the room.

As they scanned the sticky notes, Marcus leaned back

and said, "Wow... I didn't realize how innovative this product was when it first launched. I've only heard about the current problems. But this? This was kind of revolutionary, wasn't it?"

Jessica blinked. "Yeah. It really was. We worked so hard on this thing. That's why it's been so hard to let it go. It's like... it's ours." She paused. Her voice wavered just slightly. "It was our baby," she said. "We have given everything of ourselves to it." She reached for a tissue.

The room went still.

Another veteran, Sean, cleared his throat. "Okay... the ground rules said be vulnerable, so here it goes. I think I've been angry because it feels like nobody appreciates what we built. And if people don't appreciate the work, they don't appreciate us. That's what's been hard."

Tim felt the knot in his chest loosen a bit.

A newer engineer spoke up. "Sean, thank you for saying that. Honestly...I had no idea. I assumed you all didn't respect us, or didn't want to work with us because we were new. But I can see now—it's not about us. It's about your connection to this."

Another pause. Another shift.

The tension in the room softened.

Anca paused before pointing to the wall. "Take a look at what you've built here. These sticky notes are telling you something!"

The group leaned in.

Cary then asked them to cluster the sticky notes, not by color, but by theme. What patterns were emerging? What were they really seeing?

Jessica walked to the board and pointed to one cluster.

"This note says the product was the first to combine two technologies. That was our biggest innovation at the time. But now, everything else in this cluster is blue or green. I'm starting to realize... maybe that innovation isn't a strength anymore. Maybe that's what's holding us back."

No one spoke for a few seconds. Everyone just looked at the board. At each other.

Then Marcus stepped forward and added, "So maybe it's not about throwing it away. It's about evolving it."

Tim couldn't believe what he was hearing and seeing.

Collaboration. Right there. In real time.

The session ended with a small sense of progress. Not big, but *real*. Tim could feel it. Something had cracked open.

As the team left the room, there was chatter. Smiles, even laughter. Jessica and Marcus exchanged dog pictures on their phones as they walked toward their offices.

For the first time in weeks, Tim didn't feel like he was carrying the weight alone.

He didn't say much that during the facilitated session.

He just watched and learned.

He thought to himself: Maybe this is what collaboration actually looks like.

CHAPTER 3
So, What is Collaboration?

Merriam-Webster defines *collaboration* as, "The action of working with someone to create or produce something, particularly in an intellectual endeavor."

Sounds straightforward enough, right?

As we've seen from Tim's story, and likely your own experience, it's not that simple.

> ## col·lab·o·ra·tion
> ### [noun]
> ___
> The action of working with someone to produce or create something.

Collaboration goes far beyond just working on something together or sharing information. It lives at the intersection of knowledge sharing, problem-solving, decision-making, and human interaction. It's not just about the *what*; it's about the *how*, the *who*, and most importantly, the *why now*.

Tim thought back to the endless meetings he'd endured over the past month. Each one ended the same way: high tension, more confusion than clarity, and no concrete steps forward. Somewhere along the way, his organization had merged the idea of "collaboration" with the idea of "meetings."

Collaboration isn't about putting people in a room and hoping for the best.

From Projects to People to Pressure

Tim's company, like many modern organizations, has become increasingly matrixed and project-based. This means that the complexity of work has multiplied, and not just in terms of what needs to be done, but in *who* needs to be involved, and *how* to get everyone moving in the same direction.

Tim's job is no longer just about managing a project. It is about navigating a web of relationships, expectations, personalities, unspoken dynamics, old wounds, and competing ideas. It isn't just collaboration; it is high-stakes collaboration.

In today's world, that kind of collaboration is becoming more common, not less. As work becomes increasingly cross-functional, ambiguous, and human-centered, the stakes are high in terms of both emotional and organizational costs and risks.

Low-Stakes vs. High-Stakes Collaboration

At its most basic, high-stakes collaboration isn't just about doing the work, it's about doing the work while carrying the weight of everything that comes with it: interpersonal histories, dynamics, power levels, working and communication styles, assumptions, feelings, cultures, and expectations.

All in one room. All influencing the outcome. And still, somehow, the group has to move forward, productively.

No wonder Tim was overwhelmed.

When we had our discovery call with Tim, he shared with us that he was debating whether to bring the team back together. Maybe it was safer to avoid another blow-up. Maybe they could collaborate in a Google Doc instead. Or trade comments in a project management tool. Did they really *have* to be in the same room?

Our answer to him was...yes.

Because this wasn't just about re-designing a product; this was about building *alignment*. And that kind of work can't always happen behind a screen. To understand when and how to bring people together, and then what to have them do, you first need to understand the core dimensions of collaboration.

Dimensions of Collaboration

Let's say you've determined your team needs to collaborate. Great. But now the real question is:

 **What kind of collaboration are you designing for?**

To design the right kind of interaction, we've found it helpful to consider four dimensions:

 *Length of Time*
How long will the collaboration last?

Calculate time to establish expectations: How long do you anticipate needing to work together? Is it:

Short-term: One-time efforts (e.g. drafting a grant proposal, designing a slide deck

Long-term: Ongoing work (e.g. writing and publishing a book, redesigning a degree program)

 Clarity
How clear is the task at hand?

Clarity deals with how well the group understands the work to be done, and how easily that work can be accomplished. The types of tasks that a group has done before, or can easily find templates for, are clearer to everyone from the outset. These might include things like a business plan or a pitch deck for a new client. When a team takes on a task they've never done before, or that doesn't have clear outcomes, it may be more ambiguous or vague for the group.

Clarity doesn't mean the work is *easy*. It just means the group has a shared mental model of the outcome. When expectations are ambiguous or evolving, collaboration gets harder, and even more essential.

- **Clear**: Everyone understands what needs to be done, and what success looks like (e.g. crafting a business plan)

- **Ambiguous**: The goal is murky, or the path is unclear (e.g. redesigning an outdated product or creating something entirely new)

Relational Requirements
How much do relationships matter to the success of the work?

We almost always lean on relationships in our professional interactions. However, there are times when our need for an existing relationship or new relationship is shallower. For example, you may need the legal department of your organization to review a contract before it is sent to a new client. You don't necessarily need to have a strong relationship with someone in that department; part of their role in the organization, after all, is to manage risk and ensure contractual agreements are legally sound. You still need them to collaborate with you during negotiations with the client, but you don't necessarily need to make the legal counsel your new work best friend (although, let's be honest, having a friend in the legal department is never a bad idea!). On the other hand, let's say you have been tasked with helping the legal department redesign how they review contracts and support the business. In that case, you likely want to build a strong relationship with people in the legal department, and to do so, you'll need to understand their perspectives and work closely with them.

- **Low relational requirement**: You can complete the task without building or strengthening relationships (e.g. getting your policy doc reviewed by legal) because you don't need to develop a lot of trust or vulnerability with the person/people

- **High relational requirement**: You need to forge or repair connections to get the work done (e.g. redesigning a shared process across departments) because you'll need to develop a high degree of trust and vulnerability with the parties involved to get the work done

This is one of the most overlooked collaboration dimensions. If you're asking people to show up differently, stretch themselves, or take creative risks, they need to feel psychologically safe. By psychologically safe, we mean that people believe that they will not be punished or humiliated for speaking up with ideas, questions, concerns, or mistakes. This only happens when relational trust is strong

Human Complexity

What else are people bringing with them into the room?

Let's face it: humans are messy.

We hold onto past traumas; when we are proud of our work, we can become emotionally connected to it; we can hold grudges and not "jive" with people from a personal work-style or communication level.

Unfortunately when we're collaborating, we bring all of that messiness with us.

These are the "elephants in the room" that may go unseen or unacknowledged. The messier it is, the higher stakes the collaboration becomes. Understanding ahead of time which of these dynamics may be at play can help you when you're designing the type of interaction that will help the group succeed.

- **Low messiness**: No real history, healthy dynamics, flat power structure

- **High messiness**: Past trauma, emotional attachments, power imbalances, or just straight-up interpersonal tension

If human complexity exists in this interaction—and let's be honest, it usually does—you're looking at a more complex, high-stakes collaboration.

The Quick Assessment

How can you tell if you're dealing with **low-stakes** or **high-stakes** collaboration? Use the following assessment to get a quick "gut check" to help answer this question.

- If relationships need repair, or if there's visible (or invisible) messiness—*it's high stakes.*
- If the work is long-term and emotionally charged—*it's high stakes.*
- If people are protecting turf or processing past failures—*you guessed it—**high stakes.***

NOTE: Even if time and clarity are low, *one strong "yes"* in the relational or human complexity categories shifts the work toward **high-stakes collaboration**. That's why the last two dimensions are weighted more heavily.

Collaboration Dimensions Quick Assessment

Is this Low Stakes or High Stakes Collaboration?

Length of time						
Short term				Long term		
1	2	3	4	5	6	7
Clarity						
Clear expectations				Ambiguous and unclear expectations		
1	2	3	4	5	6	7
Relational Requirements*						
Low relational requirements— Don't need to form new or strengthen existing relationships; building trust isn't going to be an issue.				High relational requirements— Need to create new bonds or reinforce relationships; the need for trust and the ability to be "real" and vulnerable is high		
8	9	10	11	12	13	14
Human Complexity/Messiness*						
Not messy at all—no historical trauma, affiliations to the task, or interpersonal challenges				VERY messy—past trauma, people are emotionally attached to the task, and/or there are interpersonal challenges		
8	9	10	11	12	13	14
LOW STAKES (total scores of 4-16) HIGH STAKES (total scores of 17+)						

That's exactly where Tim was: in a high-stakes collaboration. He didn't need more meetings. He needed real collaboration: the kind designed intentionally to address complexity, build connection, and create clarity in the fog.

Luckily, designing for collaboration can be learned. And that's where we came in, and not just for Tim, but for many leaders like him. Leaders who are smart, capable, and respected...and yet still struggling with how to design for collaboration, because no one ever taught them.

We don't just teach this. We live it. We use the same tools and principles in our own work. Sometimes we nail it; sometimes we mess it up. But every time, we learn, and we design better the next time.

So what does this look like in real life?

The truth is, knowing how to *spot* a high stakes collaboration is just the beginning. The real magic is learning how to *design for it*. And to do that, it helps to see what these different types of collaboration look like in action: how they unfold, what they require, and what the outcomes can be.

To illustrate this technique, we want to share two real examples from our own consulting practice. One represents a **low-stakes collaboration**: a fast-moving, focused project with minimal messiness and clear expectations. The other is the exact opposite: a **high-stakes collaboration** that required time, emotional intelligence, trust-building, and thoughtful navigation of ambiguity and identity.

Let's start with the low-stakes one.

OUR STORY: PART 1—LOW-STAKES COLLABORATION

In 2024, we came across a fantastic grant opportunity. As soon as we read it, we thought, *This is right up our alley*. But we also knew we couldn't do it alone. Certain pieces, sure, but not the whole thing. So we looked to our network of amazing experts and doers and invited five individuals to collaborate with us.

The grant focused on bringing innovative STEM (Science, Technology, Engineering, Math) activities to underrepresented learners in the broader community to spark their interest in STEM-related careers. The submission process was simple: a few admin questions and a 500-word overview of our idea. It had to be tight, clear, and answer the WHY, WHO, HOW, and WHY NOW.

We pulled our collaborators together for a 30-minute Zoom call. During the call, we explained how we found the opportunity, why it interested us, what was required, and how we imagined we could team up. Then the ideas started flowing. One person had run a similar program with a different group. Another had a connection with a local community organization that could be our target audience. We added that we could incorporate LEGO® SERIOUS PLAY® and art-based activities to evolve the idea from STEM to STEAM.

By the end of the call, we had a solid plan, and everyone was excited. The final question: "Are you in?" resulted in a unanimous *yes*. We told them we'd follow up with a plan for how we could co-create the proposal before the deadline, which was just two weeks away.

After the call, we assessed the collaboration using our framework:

- **Length of Time:** Short and contained. We only had to focus on completing the proposal for now; if we were awarded the grant, a longer-term collaboration would follow.

- **Clarity:** Extremely clear expectations. We knew the format, word count, and evaluation criteria.

- **Relational Requirements:** Minimal. These were people we already knew. This collaboration didn't require us to deepen relationships. Instead, it focused more on tapping into existing ones.

- **Human Complexity:** None. There were no politics, power dynamics, or past drama to navigate.

It was a textbook example of low-stakes collaboration. We created a Google Doc, shared the link, and in less than a week, the proposal was written and submitted.

We didn't end up winning the grant. But when we shared that news, every person on the team responded with some version of: "That was fun—let's do it again sometime!" It was productive, energizing, and relationship-affirming. And because of that, we'd all happily work together again.

OUR STORY: PART 2—HIGH-STAKES COLLABORATION

In 2022, we conducted a qualitative research study in which we interviewed over 100 executive leaders to better understand what skills they felt were missing in leadership education. As expected, we heard things like "data-driven decision-making" and "emotional intelligence." But three findings surprised us: improvisation, collaboration, and storytelling.

As collaboration experts, we were thrilled, but also curious. Why were these three elements so important as leadership skills? More importantly, if current leaders feel like they lack these skills, how do they build them? To find out, we deep-dove into books, workshops, and classes. That's how we discovered *The Improv Mindset* by Bruce and Gail Montgomery. As luck would have it, Cary already knew Bruce. So, we reached out.

One invitation later, Bruce and Gail were in Phoenix running an improv masterclass. Afterward, the four of us sat down for what became a four-hour whiteboard session during which we pitched a wild idea: What if we collaborated to build something new that addressed all three missing leadership skills?

They were in.

That's how the seeds of *Leadership Intelligence (LQ)* were planted. Over the next 6-12 months, we had a lot of Zooms, sticky notes, and "what ifs." It was messy, uncertain, and exciting. Eventually, we piloted modules with a leadership team, and the collaboration is still ongoing.

We knew from the start this was high-stakes. Why?

- **Length of Time:** Long-term. We had jobs, lives, families. This wasn't moving fast.

- **Clarity:** Very low. We knew the outcome we wanted, but not the format, business model, or delivery method.

- **Relational Requirements:** High. We had to build new trust, fast.

- **Human Complexity:** Medium-high. Several of us were coming to the table with past collaboration trauma. We also had a mutual fear of stepping on toes, in that our businesses overlap in some areas, which meant we needed to be intentional about boundaries and credit-sharing.

So we did what we do best: we designed the collaboration. We focused on building the relationship first. This included things like visiting each other, cheering each other on, sharing stories over brunch. We used every meeting to build trust and create psychological safety. We modeled the very practices we teach.

Whether LQ becomes a breakout success or a meaningful experiment, the collaboration has been a success. Not just because of what we've built, but because of how we've built it, together.

We hope that by now, it's clear: not all collaboration is created equal. Sometimes, it's light, fast, and clean—like our short-term grant proposal. Other times, it's slow, messy, and complex—like our ongoing collaboration with Bruce and Gail. Both are valid. Both require intention. But only one of them required real design.

Once you realize you're in a high-stakes collaboration, you can't just wing it. You can't show up with a half-baked agenda, cross your fingers, and hope for alignment. That's not how it works. High-stakes collaboration is too complex, too personal, and too important to leave to chance.

 *So what does it mean to design for collaboration?*

Is it just about scheduling a meeting and having an agenda?

Nope.

It's about the process.

The Need for Collaboration Process

One of the most overlooked truths about high-stakes collaboration is this: it isn't just about *what* you're working on, it's about *how* you work together. This means that for every project, you must understand the critical difference between content and process.

- **Content** is the subject matter expertise, the idea, the product, the strategy, the thing you're trying to move forward.

- **Process** is how you engage people around that content: the structure, the flow, the format, and the conditions you create for collaboration to happen.

Here's where most well-intentioned leaders get tripped up: they are hired, promoted, or respected for being content experts. And they try to lead collaboration like they lead content: with confidence, direction, and clarity. But without a collaborative process in place, that approach often falls flat.

Just think back to Tim. He knew product design inside and out. But when he tried to lead a cross-functional team using the only process he'd ever known (i.e., his high school baseball coach's playbook) it blew up in his face. Not because he lacked intelligence or effort. But because he lacked the tools for leading a collaboration *process* designed for people, not players.

This isn't Tim's fault. Most of us were never taught how to design collaboration. We've all been led to believe we should just know how to do it. That's the *Collaboration Illusion* messing with us.

If you take nothing else from this chapter, take this:

High-stakes collaboration requires a deliberate strategy and a thoughtfully designed process. Period.

When you get this right, the benefits go way beyond completing the task at hand.

A strategic process transforms teams.

It builds trust.
It sparks hope[14].
It re-energizes cultures.

Let's take a closer look at what happens when high-stakes collaboration is done well, and why it's worth the effort.

The Positive Effects of High Stakes Collaboration Done Well

We've spent a lot of time talking about why collaboration can feel so hard and learning through Tim's story about what happens when it goes wrong. But what about when it goes right? What are the actual benefits of collaboration done well?

Some of what we're about to share comes directly from our lived experience, and these effects are backed by a growing body of research. In fact, witnessing these transformations is one of the reasons we left the comfort and stability of our traditional organizational jobs to step into the (slightly terrifying) world of consulting.

Done well, collaboration can be transformative at every level:

 Micro (individual)

 **Meso** (team)

 **Macro** (organization)

We're not saying collaboration is a cure-all. We are saying that when it's done right, it's one of the most powerful tools leaders have to unlock trust, alignment, creativity, and performance.

 ### *Encourages Psychological Safety and Enhances Team Performance*

Psychological safety and trust are often mentioned in the same breath—and for good reason. Both are foundational to high-performing teams. While they're connected, they are not the same.

Harvard scholar Amy Edmondson has significantly advanced

our understanding of what makes teams thrive. She found that psychological safety is essential for people to feel comfortable enough to take risks, voice ideas, admit mistakes, and be creative. It requires open communication, shared goals, mutual support, and respect. When these conditions exist, team members can show up fully and contribute meaningfully[15].

Trust, on the other hand, is about reliability and predictability. It's the belief that you can count on others to follow through, act with integrity, and behave consistently[16][17]. **If psychological safety is about emotional permission, then trust is about relational confidence.**

Here's the tricky part: psychological safety can sometimes be sparked quickly, but trust takes time and repetition. Both can be built...but both can also be broken instantly.

So how do you *build* them? What does it actually look like to "do" psychological safety or create trust in real-world team settings?

This is where the collaboration process becomes essential.

There's often a chicken-and-egg dilemma here. Many people assume you need trust and safety before you can collaborate effectively. But what we've found, time and again, is that when a solid collaboration process is in place, *psychological safety* and *trust* can be built through the work.

In other words, engaging in a well-designed, high-stakes collaboration can actually *help to build* psychological safety and trust. As teams tackle challenges together, make progress, hit bumps, regroup, and move forward, they start to build that emotional glue. They develop trust not just from words, but from shared experience.

Once that emotional and relational lift is created, it doesn't just fade. Teams carry it forward into their ongoing work. They communicate more openly. They recover from conflict faster. They perform better. We've seen this in dozens of groups—and it's supported by a growing body of research[18].

 ### *Improves optimism, hope, and resilience*

In addition to building trust and psychological safety, successful high-stakes collaboration can enhance something equally vital: psychological capital[19]. Specifically, it can increase a team's shared sense of optimism, hope, and resilience. These terms are often used interchangeably, but they each represent unique psychological strengths, and successful collaboration can nurture all three.

Optimism is the belief that positive outcomes are possible. It's often viewed as a personal trait, and something you either have or you don't. Are you a "glass half full" person or a "glass half empty" one? But optimism is not fixed. Researchers like Carol Dweck and Martin Seligman have shown that a growth mindset and optimistic outlook can be learned, modeled, and even *spread*[20]. In fact, further research shows that optimism is contagious: when one team member expresses confidence and enthusiasm, it can influence the emotional tone of the whole group[21] .

Hope, while related to optimism, is more than a feeling. It's also a cognitive and motivational process. Hope includes not just seeing a better future, it involves believing it can be reached *and* developing pathways to get there. According to researcher C.R. Snyder, hope is built on two core ingredients: the will (motivation) and the way (strategy)[22]. Hope is active. It's a force that fuels action. And more than that, hope can be created, or crushed, by how well groups collaborate together to move ideas forward[23].

Resilience is the ability to bounce back after failure, adapt under pressure, and try again after things fall apart. Hope and resilience are closely connected. When we feel hopeful, we are more likely to persist through challenges. When we've been knocked down, resilience helps us get back up and try a new approach. That cycle—envisioning a better future, hitting roadblocks, and trying again—is at the heart of collaborative work[24].

When teams engage in high-stakes collaboration, they often co-create not just solutions, but shared optimism and hope. Together, they imagine a better outcome, chart a course toward it, and support one another through obstacles and setbacks[25]. When, inevitably, failure shows up, these same teams build resilience by learning, adapting, and pressing forward.

This connection between failure, resilience, and creativity is well documented. In fact, failure is often a prerequisite for innovation[26]. The more comfortable teams become with failing forward together, the more creatively they can respond to uncertainty and complexity.

Optimism, hope, and resilience may be distinct, but they're deeply intertwined. When built intentionally through high-stakes collaboration, they become reinforcing loops: strengthening the team's mindset, adaptability, and momentum over time.

 ### *Builds relationships and strengthens network ties*

Given its impact on psychological safety and trust, it should come as no surprise that successful collaboration strengthens relationships, and not just within teams, but across entire organizations. In fact, one of the lesser-discussed benefits of collaboration is how effectively it breaks down silos. It opens up pathways between departments, job functions, and power levels by bridging gaps that otherwise stay firmly in place.

The impact doesn't stop with strengthening the relationships among close teammates. Strong collaboration can also enhance what sociologists call *weak ties*, which are connections between people who don't interact often or directly. Research on structural holes and the strength of weak ties shows us that these looser relationships can actually be just as important, if not more important, for spreading ideas, sparking innovation, and improving resilience within an organization[27]. In other words: the more you collaborate across boundaries, the more connected and adaptable your organization becomes.

 ### *Increases collaboration, organizational attachment and employee engagement*

Now let's zoom out even further. When collaboration is done well (and we don't mean performative collaboration, but real, meaningful, co-creative work) it increases more than just trust or innovation. It increases attachment. People begin to feel more connected to their teams, to their organizations, and to the work itself.

This makes sense when you think about it. Collaboration allows people to bring more of themselves into the room. They get to use their voices, share their ideas, and contribute to something that feels meaningful. Research from Meyer and Allen[28] shows that this kind of experience builds organizational commitment. When people feel valued, respected, and like their work matters, their engagement naturally increases. Research on engagement further emphasizes that people are more emotionally and cognitively invested when they feel psychological safety and purpose[29].

Remember the sobering picture from earlier, of how Tim's team seemed to disconnect after their poor collaboration experiences? Gallup's 2024 report shows that engagement levels across the workforce remain worryingly low[30]. In fact, one of the few proven drivers of increased engagement is—you guessed it!—collaboration. Collaborative environments correlate strongly with higher levels of job engagement and organizational citizenship behavior[31].

Of course, we're not saying that collaboration is a panacea *(a.k.a., a solution or remedy for all difficulties).* It won't magically fix every organizational issue or interpersonal challenge.

But we are saying this: when done well, and when it's designed with intention and guided by good process, collaboration unlocks benefits that ripple outward.

The gains might not always be easy to quantify, but they are real. They're why we call this kind of collaboration **high stakes**: because the potential for deep, lasting, positive impact is just that powerful.

ANCA'S STORY: PART 2—THE FACULTY MEETING

Remember the earlier story about the 15 faculty members who came together to build a new interdisciplinary degree, and how disastrous that 60-minute virtual meeting was? Afterward, I approached the associate dean, John, and asked what he thought. Without hesitation, he said, "I have no idea what to do. That was horrible."

So, I offered a suggestion: "Would it be okay if I facilitated the next meeting? I can bring in some structure, design, and activities to help the group have a more collaborative conversation."

He said yes. And that's exactly what I did.

I designed the next 60-minute interaction with intention. Knowing how people would likely walk in, and where I needed to help them get by the time they walked out, I applied the principles of collaboration I'd been learning and practicing and built a structure that gave everyone space to speak, listen, and co-create.

Here's how: Before the meeting, which was going to be held digitally over Zoom, I created a simple grid in a shared Google Doc. Each row represented a critical skill, and each column could capture courses that taught that skill. When the group arrived, I didn't start with open discussion (which had failed last time). Instead, I gave them individual time to reflect and type into the document silently. Each person listed the top 4-5 skills they believed were foundational to the new degree and matched those to current courses that supported them.

Once everyone had contributed, I asked them to cluster

the skills by grouping similar ideas and surfacing the strongest themes. Then they did the same for the courses. As the group worked together to sort and synthesize, a clear set of core skills emerged, along with a shared understanding of how existing courses mapped to those skills.

For the first time, the conversation wasn't dominated by the loudest voice. There was no bickering or power struggles. Just focused collaboration. We only paused to briefly discuss a few outliers, and the group easily agreed that those topics were still valuable, just better suited as electives.

In just one hour, the group moved from disjointed and combative to aligned and engaged. They listened to one another, offered ideas, found common ground, and designed the skeleton of a degree they were all genuinely excited about.

As people were leaving, I overheard someone say, "That was such a good meeting!"

Let's not forget: this was the same group that, just one week earlier, had spent an hour name-calling and shutting each other down. And now? They were walking out the door smiling, having *collaborated* well, and feeling good about it.

The Need for a Facilitator or Process Guide

Several key elements in Anca's story helped turn a tense, high-stakes meeting into a productive and energizing collaboration:

She asked for permission to facilitate the next meeting.

She applied core principles of collaboration to intentionally design the experience.

She structured the interaction with purpose, by choosing activities that supported a clear outcome.

None of it happened by accident. It was thoughtful, deliberate, and grounded in process.

In the chapters that follow, we'll break down each of these elements and show how you can bring the same level of intention and structure to your own high-stakes collaborations.

Chapter 3
Done!

Learning to See Differently

In truth, Tim hadn't expected much from that first session with us and the team. He thought we might try to mediate, smooth things over, maybe lay down a few rules about how people should behave. But instead, we had done something... different. Strange, even. We didn't start with the problem. We didn't rush to solutions.

We began by asking them to reflect on what had been: what had gone well, where challenges still lingered, and where they saw opportunities ahead. With that, we helped the group build a shared language. We invited them to share about themselves, and through that, learn about each other.

And people actually answered.

Not everyone, not all at once. But something cracked open. Even Jessica, who had stormed out of the "Coach Jefferson" meeting, spoke with real honesty. So did Marcus. The engineers still didn't agree on everything, but they were no longer locked in opposition. The atmosphere had shifted.

That evening, Tim sat in his car, engine off, staring at the empty parking lot. He replayed the session in his mind; not because it was perfect, but because something was different. And he realized that while the tension wasn't gone, it had softened. For the first time in weeks, it didn't feel like him vs. them.

It felt like maybe, just maybe, it could be "us".

At the next session, we tried something they didn't expect.

We dimmed the lights, projected a piece of abstract artwork onto the wall, and then Anca said: "Let's take a moment to look at this piece of art. Then I'll ask a few questions. There are no right or wrong answers here. Just share what you notice."

Parade (diptych) by Mequitta Ahuja 2007

They looked up at the image: a vivid, two-panel painting. One side was bright, textured with splashes and streaks of color. The other showed a woman walking barefoot, seemingly emerging from a chaotic tangle of dark brushstrokes and color explosions behind her.

"Okay," Anca said. "What's going on in this image?"

Silence.

Then someone ventured:

"It looks like she's stepping out of the mess. Like... escaping."

Anca listened and said, "So you see a figure, who you

believe is female, and that figure looks like she is moving, or 'escaping,' as you said, from mess into "not mess." What do you see that makes you say 'mess'?"

"Just...the dark behind her. All the colors and lines feel like a mess, like this tangled web of chaos. And her posture feels...determined."

Anca pointed to the painting and said, "So to you, the left panel feels like the mess, and you said it is the lines and colors and arrangement of it that feels messy or chaotic, and the figure's body posture looks determined and is moving away from the left panel—the messiness. Thank you. What more can we find?"

Another voice jumped in, "I see her walking into it. Maybe she doesn't even know what's coming."

Anca said, "So, to you, maybe it is the opposite of what was just shared. Instead of walking away from messiness, she is walking into it. I also heard that you get the sense of the figure being unsure or uncertain of what is ahead."

Anca smiled as the speaker nodded before asking, "What do you see that makes you say the figure is uncertain of what is ahead?"

"I would say it is the direction of the figure, and how that energy seems to hit her head. Like she's about to be overwhelmed. But now that I look at it more, maybe it's not hitting her. Maybe it is more like she is absorbing it. Like the chaos is part of her creativity."

Reflecting back, Anca said, "At first, it was the directions and energy the figure was moving with that made you say 'uncertain,' but having looked at it longer, it sounds like you might be changing your mind from seeing the figure walking into uncertainty to absorbing it. And maybe it is not uncertainty but perhaps chaos and a relationship between chaos and creativity." She continued, "What more can we find?"

The group continued their analysis. Some saw trauma; others saw resilience. Some saw forward motion; others saw recklessness. No one interrupted. No one corrected. People asked questions, made connections, and, most importantly, they listened.

Then Tim spoke. "I see conflict. Everything's pulling in different directions. But she's still moving forward."

No one argued. A few people nodded. Anca repeatedly asked, listened, paraphrased, and prodded for deeper analysis and justification by asking: "What more can we find?"

Twenty minutes in and the conversation kept unfolding. They weren't talking about the product, or the team, or who was "right." It was about learning to look at the same thing from different lenses.

To pause.

To stay curious.

Afterward, Anca guided the group into reflection:

"Before we wrap up," she said, "I have three questions. Take a moment to think about your answers."

1. "How did you experience yourself in that activity?"
2. "How did you experience me as the facilitator?"
3. "How might this relate to your collaborative work here?"

The room got quiet again, but it was a different kind of quiet. Reflective. Open. A few people stared at the floor. Others scribbled thoughts in the margins of their notebooks.

Jessica was the first to speak, "I realized I wasn't listening before. I was just...defending. In this activity, I didn't have to defend anything. I just got to look. And it reminded me that other people aren't the enemy—they're just seeing something different."

Marcus followed, saying slowly, "I kept trying to be right. To win. But this helped me see how narrow that makes things. There's more going on here than I've been willing to look at."

Tim nodded, then added something unexpected, "The way you held the space, it made it easier to speak. You didn't push. You didn't try to steer us anywhere. You just... let us look. And somehow, that made it safer."

Jessica chimed in again, "Yeah, it felt... neutral. Like you weren't judging our answers, just helping us hear ourselves and each other."

Anca smiled, "Thank you."

The group wasn't "fixed." But something had cracked open again, and even wider this time. Less tension. More space. More seeing.

As the room cleared for a break, Tim lingered behind.

"I think I've been doing this wrong," he said. "Not because I didn't care. I just...didn't know there was another way."

We nodded.

"There is," we told him. "And you don't have to figure it out alone."

That was the moment everything started to change. Not with a grand solution, not with a roadmap or strategy deck, but in a shift in how they saw each other.

Together, they were learning to see differently.

What is Visual Thinking Strategies (VTS)?

A method for slowing down, listening deeper, and seeing more

Visual Thinking Strategies (VTS) is a research-based facilitation method developed by cognitive psychologist Abigail Housen and museum educator Philip Yenawine. Originally used to teach art interpretation, it has become a powerful tool for enhancing communication, critical thinking, and collaborative learning across fields—from classrooms to boardrooms.

At its core, VTS invites a group to interpret an image together using just **three open-ended questions**:

1. What's going on in this image?
2. What do you see that makes you say that?
3. What more can we find?

The facilitator doesn't confirm or correct. Instead, they paraphrase responses neutrally, link comments when appropriate, and continue asking these questions. The process slows people down, shifts them out of "debate mode," and helps them engage with nuance, ambiguity, and multiple perspectives.

VTS isn't about art. It's about awareness. It builds the muscle of collaborative inquiry through listening without rushing to judgment, asking better questions, and allowing truth to emerge from dialogue instead of dictation.

We use VTS in our work because it models the kind of thinking collaboration demands: curiosity, humility, empathy, and space for multiple truths.

 Want to explore more?

Check out The Hailey Group and the work of **Dabney Hailey**, who brings VTS into leadership, strategy, and organizational transformation work. Her practice shows how structured, image-based dialogue can unlock clarity and connection in even the most complex environments.

CHAPTER 4

The Facilitator as Process Guide

Facilitators guide a group through a collaborative process, especially when the stakes are high. They bring knowledge, experience, and a toolbox of strategies to help groups work through complexity, navigate tough dynamics, and align around shared goals.

Facilitators are collaboration experts.

They're equipped to design and guide interactions that move a group forward. They know how to manage tension, elevate quieter voices, ask better questions, and shift the energy in the room. That's why organizations bring them in when collaboration is

Facilitator

Expert that focuses on the process of collaboration and acts like a guide of conversations

Group

People (or experts) with content knowledge & expertise needing to come together to collaborate

difficult, or when it's simply too important to leave to chance.

You might think facilitation is a relatively new concept, but it's been around for a long time.

In fact, many indigenous cultures practiced early forms of facilitation. One of the earliest and simplest tools was the *talking stick*, passed from person to person to indicate who had the uninterrupted opportunity to speak. It ensured one voice was heard at a time, and that everyone listened with intention. The talking stick didn't just manage turn-taking. This simple tool created safety, respect, and focus. These principles still sit at the heart of good facilitation principles today.

In the mid-20th century, the field began to formalize. Thought leaders like L. David Lumsdaine, Roger Schwarz, and Sam Kaner helped shape facilitation as a professional practice, drawing from disciplines like psychology, organizational development, and conflict resolution.

In other words, becoming skilled in the *process* of collaboration is what facilitation is all about.

At this point, you might be wondering what we actually did with Tim and his team. How did we go from a group on the verge of falling apart to one that began to trust, engage, and collaborate again? We'll share all the details (promise!), but first—a quick note.

Becoming a skilled facilitator takes time. Most facilitators invest in learning specific methods and tools. These tools include things like design thinking, human-centered design, liberating structures, appreciative inquiry, futures thinking, and more. Facilitators then spend years practicing, adapting, and refining their approach through trial and error.

We've spent a lot of time (and money!) doing exactly that: learning, experimenting, building a diverse toolkit, and even creating our own facilitation framework. We also noticed that all of these facilitation and collaboration processes rest on a set of foundational principles. But we know not everyone wants to become a professional facilitator, and also, not everyone has the time, interest, or budget to bring in outside collaboration experts.

That's why we wrote this book. We want to share the foundational principles underlying great collaboration processes and help everyone understand how to be better collaborators.

Our goal isn't to turn you into a professional facilitator (although, if that's your dream, we can help with that and point you in a starting direction) . Instead, this book will give you a set of foundational principles and simple, practical strategies that can help you become a *better collaborator*, starting right now.

Because even small shifts can make a big difference.

 **One more thing**, speaking from experience: once you begin to apply these ideas, people may start noticing. They might say things like, "You're really good at this," or "Can you help us with this meeting?" You might get pulled into more conversations and projects— not because you asked for it, but because good collaborators are magnetic.

Consider this your thoughtful (and slightly cheeky) warning.

Chapter 4
Done!

TIM'S STORY: PART 5

Stepping Into the Role

Something had shifted.

We'd led the group through five sessions. Not just meetings, but real, designed collaborations. They'd wrestled with competing perspectives, rebuilt just enough trust to take creative risks, and developed four conceptual redesigns for their product. There was still work ahead, of course. But now, for the first time in months, they had momentum. They had clarity. They had hope.

Most importantly, they had each other.

As we wrapped the fifth session, we pulled Tim aside.

"You're ready," we said.

He furrowed his brow. "Ready for what?"

"To lead the next one."

Tim looked uncertain. "You mean...like, fully?"

"Fully. We'll be there, but in the background as silent support. We'll help you design the session, prep the structure, and think through the process. But you'll run it."

He didn't say anything right away. He just nodded slowly, the kind of nod that says, "I'm not sure I believe it, but I trust you believe it."

The following week, the team gathered around the same

table. But this time, Tim stood at the front.

He opened with calm clarity: "We've made a lot of progress together. You've helped shape four solid directions for this redesign. Today, we're going to dig deeper, by getting specific, getting tactical, and mapping out next steps. We'll be using the same process we've been practicing, and I'll be your guide for this one."

He wasn't pretending to be an expert. He wasn't trying to be someone else. He was a more present, intentional version of himself. The group responded. Jessica asked questions without defensiveness. Marcus offered critique without taking over. People built on each other's ideas. They debated, joked, and even disagreed, but it was all done productively.

And we stayed silent, just as we'd promised.

At one point, when the discussion hit a snag, Tim paused and said, *"Let's slow this down. What are we really trying to decide here?"* Then he gave them a moment to let the silence work. And someone picked up the thread.

They were doing it on their own.

After the session, Tim circled back with us.

"I can't believe how different that felt," he said. "I wasn't forcing anything. I was holding space."

We smiled. "Exactly."

He looked at the whiteboard, covered in sketches and scribbles, and shook his head with a grin. "You know what's funny? I used to think collaboration was about making sure everything stayed on track. Now I see it's about knowing when to guide, when to pause, and when to let the group lead."

Tim didn't just learn a new set of tools; he stepped into a new way of leading. And what made it possible wasn't magic; it was a series of guiding principles, practiced with intention and shared with care.

CHAPTER 5
Principles of Collaboration

At this point, we've helped hundreds, maybe even thousands, of people navigate high-stakes collaborations. As designers and facilitators, we're constantly paying attention to the process of collaboration: What works? What doesn't? What holds up across contexts, cultures, industries?

One thing we've learned: the messier the situation, the more structure and intention it requires.

Remember the "human complexity and messiness" dimension from Chapter 3? The more emotion, history, and unspoken tension in the room, the more your collaboration process needs clarity, safety, and care. But messiness isn't always obvious at first glance.

Here are a few signs it might be lurking under the surface:

- People are making assumptions—about each other, the topic, or who knows what
- No one wants to be the first to speak up or admit uncertainty
- There's a fear of conflict—or even a fear of emotion
- There's an "elephant in the room" that everyone sees but no one names
- The group has tried to collaborate before—and failed. Now they're skeptical

These are all signals. Not signs to run away, but signs that you need a different approach, and one that is built on principles, not personality. Because when collaboration goes well, it might *feel* like magic...but it's not. It's the result of a set of foundational principles, practiced with care.

Here's the thing: *These principles aren't rocket science.* In fact, they're things we all once knew how to do.

As children, we asked "why" relentlessly. We stayed curious. We played. We admitted when we didn't know something. But somewhere along the way, many of these behaviors were trained out of us, and deemed as being unprofessional, inefficient, or just "too much."

Think of this chapter as a return: A return to the foundational behaviors that make human collaboration work. A reminder of what we *already know*, deep down. This is your invitation to return to these principles. Or, if these strike you as being entirely new, this is your invitation to begin practicing them.

Foundational Principles of Great Collaboration

We've distilled what we've learned into **six core principles**. These are the bedrock of great collaboration, especially when the stakes are high, the people are messy, and the path forward isn't clear.

Foundational Principles of Great Collaboration

1. Make the abstract clear
2. Stop assuming
3. Just say it
4. Slow down to speed up
5. Walk away with something actionable
6. Plan to pivot

You'll see these again and again in the pages to come, because they're not just nice ideas, they're practices. You can build on them. You can teach them. And you can use them as a compass when collaboration gets tough.

Good collaborators have figured out ways to bring these principles to life, and we're going to share with you what some of them look like in action.

Let's walk through each one.

 ### *Make the Abstract Clear*

High-stakes collaboration is often complex and ambiguous. This means you're usually working with concepts or ideas that are difficult to define and even harder to get on the same page about.

Making the abstract clear means bringing these ideas out of your head and into the world, by writing them down, drawing them, mapping them, or building them. The goal is to move from vague thoughts to shared visual representations.

 *See It in Action*

Let's look at two versions of the same scenario to see what this principle looks like in practice.

Example A: Not making the abstract clear

A school district leadership team is meeting to discuss "flexible learning opportunities" for high schoolers. But the phrase means different things to different people: electives, scheduling, online delivery, instructor qualifications, etc.

The meeting agenda? "Go around and share your thoughts, then come to consensus. "What happens? Everyone talks. No one agrees. The group spirals into a debate about definitions and terminology. Nothing gets decided. Everyone leaves frustrated.

Example B: Making the abstract clear

Same team, same topic (a school district leadership team gathers to discuss flexible learning opportunities for high schoolers), but this time, they walk in to find whiteboards, markers, and sticky notes.

Each person starts by jotting down what they mean by "flexible learning." The notes go on the board. Together, they group similar ideas, call out differences, and build a shared map.

One person says, "I hadn't thought of it like that." Another adds more ideas. Soon, they're co-creating a collective understanding.

Same hour, totally different outcome.

What's Happening Behind the Scenes?

When we make abstract ideas visual, especially with sticky notes, we tap into a set of powerful cognitive strategies:

- **Externalization of thought**: Getting ideas out of your head and into the physical world

- **Concrete representation**: Turning an idea into something others can see and engage with

- **Cognitive clarity**: Forced brevity (hello, 3"x3") means you have to distill and clarify your thoughts

Sticky notes are more than paper squares—they're collaboration tools. They allow people to express fuzzy ideas, see where perspectives overlap or diverge, and build something together.

Flexible Learning Looks Like:

The Power of Anonymity

Sticky notes also provide a degree of **anonymity**, especially when using digital tools like Mural, Miro, or Jamboard. Anonymity matters, particularly in emotionally charged or high-stakes conversations. When people don't feel singled out, they're more likely to be honest.

Important caveat: this isn't a license to be a jerk. It's about offering psychological safety to share candidly, without fear of being judged or penalized.

"Mine" Becomes "Ours"

Something subtle and important happens when you put your sticky note on the wall: It becomes *part of the group's conversation.*

Ideas stop being personal and start being communal. That opens up the space for something called chaining, wherein one person's thought sparks another's, and connections emerge that no individual could have generated alone[32].

Someone might glance at a sticky note and think, *I didn't realize you felt that way, too.*

That's not just idea-sharing. That's relationship-building.

TIM'S TEAM: STICKY NOTES AND BREAK-THROUGHS

With Tim's team, we decided early on: every contribution would be written. No exceptions. Whether it was an idea, a comment, a question, or an objection, everything had to be captured.

We used Mural, even for in-person sessions. Laptops open, sticky notes flying. At first, the team resisted. They were used to "just talking." But we gently insisted. If someone spoke an idea, we'd pause and either ask them to write it or offer to capture it for them.

We also used giant posters, markers, and drawing activities...whatever materials helped them get ideas out of their heads and into a shared space. Over time, this practice stopped feeling strange. It became a norm.

Eventually, that norm helped surface one of the biggest breakthroughs:

During an audience-mapping session, the team was trying to understand who the flagship product was really for. They wrote out all the different user groups they were trying to serve: technical teams, business leaders, nonprofit users, individual creators...

That's when one of the veteran engineers spoke up:

"I see the problem now. We're trying to be everything to everyone. And that means we're becoming nothing special to anyone."

The room fell quiet. Someone drew a big pink sticky note and wrote that quote in bold letters with an exclamation mark. That moment became an anchor for their work ahead.

It didn't come from debate. It came from shared visualization. That's what this principle makes possible.

Summary of Principle 1: Make the Abstract Clear

Let's recap what we've learned about this principle:

- ☑ When you're dealing with ambiguity, make it visible. Don't just talk about ideas—**show** them.

- ☑ Sticky notes (physical or digital) are a powerful way to clarify thought and surface shared understanding.

- ☑ Writing things down enables people to express things they might struggle to say out loud.

- ☑ Once shared, ideas become **group property**, which sparks connection, sharing, and trust.

- ☑ Anonymity (especially in digital spaces) can help surface truths people might otherwise withhold.

When in doubt—use sticky notes.

When still in doubt—use more sticky notes.

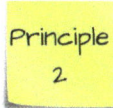

Stop Assuming

We've all heard the old saying, "Assuming makes an ass out of you and me." And yet, especially in group collaboration, we do it all the time:

- We assume we're all on the same page.
- We assume we're ready and able to collaborate.
- We assume we understand what the topic is, how we'll work together, or why certain people are even in the room.

Sound familiar?

Many of these assumptions stem from *The Collaboration Illusion*: the belief that because we can communicate, we should automatically be good at collaboration. But as anyone who's been in a messy meeting knows, that's just not true.

A Cautionary Tale: The Abilene Paradox

One of the most well-known stories about group assumptions comes from Jerry B. Harvey's "Abilene Paradox," a parable written in 1988 to describe why groups sometimes make decisions that no one actually wants.

In the story, a family is enjoying a hot summer afternoon on the porch in Abilene, Texas. One person casually suggests they take a long, uncomfortable car ride to a restaurant in the next town. Even though no one likes the idea (dust storm, 100+ degree weather, no AC), everyone goes along with it because each person assumes the others want to go.

The result? A miserable trip that nobody wanted.

Why did it happen? Because no one asked the obvious question: "Do we actually want to do this?"

Why Assumptions Persist

Assumptions are often a shortcut. Maybe we don't want to be the one asking the "dumb question." Maybe we assume everyone else is aligned, and we're the only outsider. Or going back to social pain, we don't want to become the outsider in our group by going against what we assume is the group's decisions. Or maybe we've worked together for so long that we believe we already know how the others think, feel, or will respond.

But when assumptions go unchecked, they erode clarity, build resentment, and kill collaboration before it even starts.

To counter this, we need to do something radical: be explicit. About everything.

 *See It in Action*

Let's look at how this principle plays out with a group of volunteers working to support the mental health and wellbeing of healthcare providers. The group includes people who know each other, people who don't, people who care deeply about the mission, and people who have deeply personal and painful stories.

At their first meeting, things go off the rails quickly. Kyle, the most senior person in the room, assumes he should take charge. Two of his colleagues defer to him. Carla, a female executive, feels sidelined and suspects gender bias. Carlos assumes the group should be talking about structural changes like editing admission language in medical board tests, not transformations at the individual level, like practicing mindfulness or peer coaching. No one has the same idea of what "supporting mental health" means.

By the end of the meeting, half the room is confused. The other half is angry.

Now let's rewind and imagine how the meeting would go if they *stopped assuming*.

Juliana, who has some training in high-stakes collaboration, offers to guide the process. She asks everyone to introduce themselves with three things:

1. Name and where they work
2. Why this cause matters to them
3. How they hope to contribute

The answers are moving: personal stories, teary eyes, shared values. Connection begins to form.

Next, Juliana invites the group to set ground rules. She offers a few examples like "listen to understand" and "assume positive intent," then lets the group build their own list. They agree to adopt these rules going forward.

Then, each person answers basic but powerful questions: Who are we trying to help? What are we trying to achieve? Why does this matter? They write their answers on sticky notes and cluster them into themes.

By the end, they have a shared purpose, a clear sense of who's in the room, and how they'll work together. No one is assuming; instead, they're actually aligning.

What Happened?

In the first version, they fell into four common traps:

- Assuming they knew each other's roles or perspectives
- Assuming they knew how to act together
- Assuming they were aligned on the problem
- Assuming everyone was emotionally ready to collaborate

Juliana helped the group slow down and surface those assumptions through intentional design. She used introductions, ground rules, and structured prompts to create clarity and connection.

Here's a quick table of how assumptions were countered:

ASSUMPTION	STRUCTURED EXERCISE
We know each other's roles	Introductions + contribution prompt
We know how to act together	Create ground rules
We're aligned on the topic	5Ws exercise on sticky notes (who, what, where, when, how, and why of the topic)
We're ready to contribute	Personal connection-sharing

Ground Rules to Start

As the late psychologist Judith Glaser said: "Words create worlds." Ground rules aren't fluff. They create psychological safety and shared expectations. Here are a few we use often:

- **Safe Space**: This is a safe space for sharing. The stories and personal things people share in this space will stay here; we can take the learnings and lessons that impacted us personally with us.

- **Listen to understand, not to judge**: When someone shares something, I will first seek to listen to understand them and their perspective, and not automatically jump to judging or evaluating the thought or person

- **Assume positive intent**: I believe that everyone is here with a positive intent to contribute

- **No abbreviations** (this one is especially important if members of the group are not part of the same team): I will spell out acronyms rather than assume everyone is using the same dictionary or language

- **Stay engaged** (this one is especially important in digital meetings): To the best of my ability, I will stay present and focused on this interaction

- **Be vulnerable**: I will be open to sharing my emotions and being honest with my thoughts and reflections and how something is impacting me

Let the group add or edit. Different cultures and contexts may shape what's needed.

TIM'S TEAM

Remember Jessica? Tim had warned us she'd walked out of the last meeting and was skeptical of the whole process. But when we opened with our usual ground rules and asked, "What's an ordinary moment that brings you joy?" something shifted. Jessica mentioned walking her dog. Marcus said he did too. They smiled. The room softened.

Then, we moved into a Rose-Thorn-Bud activity. Each engineer shared what they loved about the flagship product (rose), what wasn't working (thorn), and new ideas (bud). Sticky notes went up. Stories came out. The product wasn't just a product—it was their baby. And now they were grieving the idea of changing, or even losing, it.

The space, which was created by the ground rules, reinforced by prompts, protected by process, gave people the safety to say what they hadn't before. Assumptions were named and dismantled. New understandings formed. One person's vulnerability made space for another's.

Jessica teared up. Sean admitted his anger. A new engineer shared that he'd assumed the veterans didn't respect him. "Now I see what I didn't know," he said. "I didn't realize how much this product meant to you."

And just like that, the group took a breath. Together.

Summary of Principle 2: Stop Assuming

Assumptions are normal, but dangerous in collaboration. Common assumptions include:

- We know each other's roles
- We know how to behave together
- We're aligned on what we're doing
- Everyone's emotionally ready to participate

Counter assumptions with intentional structure: introductions, ground rules, shared definitions. And when in doubt?

- Slow down
- Ask the question
- Name the elephant

Because collaboration thrives when we stop assuming—and start getting curious.

 **Just Say It**

We are shaped by our experiences and the world around us. The households and cultures we grow up in, the social situations we navigate, and the behavioral norms we absorb all guide how we interpret the world and what we believe is "good" or "appropriate" behavior.

As mothers, we've watched our children move through this process in real time. Anca's six-year-old delights equally in sharing her opinions and defending why they're not just valid, but superior. Cary's twelve-year-old, on the other hand, has already started editing himself. He now scans the room, checking for approval before sharing anything personal or vulnerable.

It happens to most of us. In the world of work, we're often

expected to be composed, contained, and professional. That usually means limiting emotional expression, deferring to authority, and avoiding conflict. We learn to hold back. To protect our reputations. To stay safe.

But here's the challenge: real collaboration asks us to do the opposite. It asks us to speak up. To share what we feel to be true. To say the things that need to be said, even when they're uncomfortable.

Of course, this is easier said than done. Most of us will only speak our minds when we feel safe; when we trust that our words won't be punished, dismissed, or misunderstood. That sense of security is what Edmondson calls psychological safety: a belief that you can take interpersonal risks without fear of negative consequences. As we shared earlier, when done well, high-stakes collaboration can actually build psychological safety and trust. But only if the right foundation is in place.

This principle builds directly on the two that came before. When we *make the abstract clear* (Principle 1) and *stop assuming* by being explicit about expectations and shared understanding (Principle 2), we begin to create the kind of environment where people feel safe enough to speak honestly. That's what enables Principle 3: *Saying the thing that needs to be said.*

It's not as simple as "1 + 2 = 3," but there's a reason these principles build on each other. Jumping straight to "just saying it" without establishing clarity or trust can do more harm than good. But when the groundwork is there, we can begin to design collaboration processes that actively invite honesty, vulnerability, and truth-telling. Let's look at what this can look like in action through three brief scenarios:

1. A group that hasn't embraced any of the principles
2. A group that tries to "just say it" without building the foundation
3. A group that puts all three principles into practice

SCENARIO 1
STATUS QUO (A.K.A., NO PRINCIPLES ADOPTED)

The office team of a small company has gathered to discuss issues with their purchasing policies.

The company, which creates supply kits for teachers and students, has expanded rapidly into the homeschool and online learning markets since the pandemic.

That growth has strained the small team, and especially Helen, the longtime employee handling all purchasing. Orders are delayed. Customers are frustrated. Something needs to change.

Present at the meeting are the company president, vice president, head of operations, office director, Helen (the purchasing lead), and the office manager.

Sonja, the president, jumps right in. "Why are these orders backed up? What needs to change?"

Helen shifts in her seat, eyes downcast. Russ, the office director, pulls out the company's purchasing policy and suggests a few minor edits.

He also says the sales reps should be retrained on how to place orders. Everyone reads in silence. A few suggestions are made. Helen doesn't speak.

No one asks for her input. No one names what's going unsaid.

As the meeting wraps and everyone gets up for lunch, Helen quietly slips out. She doesn't return.

A few wording changes are eventually made, but nothing significant changes. Orders continue to back up. Tensions rise. Accusations are made.

Not long after, Helen submits her retirement paperwork and leaves the company.

SCENARIO 2
JUST SAY IT... WITHOUT THE FOUNDATION

Same team. Same issue. But this time, when Sonja asks why orders are delayed, Office Director Russ jumps in with what everyone's been thinking.

"There's just too much volume for one person to handle," he says. "Honestly, we should probably hire someone to help Helen. She's probably counting down the days to retirement anyway!"

He tries to lighten the comment with a chuckle.

The room goes silent.

Helen glares around the table. "Is that what you all think? That I'm old and slow?"

People scramble to recover; they're talking over one another, trying to explain, backpedal, and soothe.

Helen stands up and walks out.

Russ follows her to apologize, and she eventually returns, but the mood has shifted. The meeting ends early.

Later, Sonja calls Russ into her office. She tells him to be more mindful of people's emotions, and then asks him to put together a proposal for hiring a purchasing assistant.

The new hire helps. Orders speed up.

But the rupture between Helen and Russ never fully heals.

When Helen retires nine months later, the team is right right back where they started: orders back up, stress mounts, and no clear solution is in place.

SCENARIO 3
PRACTICING ALL THREE PRINCIPLES

This time, the meeting starts differently.

Russ opens by setting some "ground rules" for the session. Then he invites everyone to share a simple joy from their weekend.

Next, he turns to Helen.

"Helen," he says, "you're our purchasing expert. Can you walk us through what happens when an order comes in, from start to finish? I really want to understand the process before we make any decisions."

There's a pause.

Helen stares at the table, then lifts her head. Her voice shakes.

"I feel like everyone thinks this is my fault. I'm doing the best I can."

Russ doesn't rush to soothe Helen. He doesn't deflect

Instead, he empathetically rephrases, "You're sharing that it feels like it's your fault—and that you're doing your best. And I can also see that it is making you sad."

Helen nods. "Yes. It makes me feel guilty."

Russ says gently, "Let's map the process out together. Show us where it gets hard. We'll figure it out as a team."

Helen picks up some sticky notes and begins mapping the order flow. The team asks questions. Slowly, a picture emerges. The problem isn't Helen.

The problem is the process: each order requires three separate approvals before Helen can do anything. That bottleneck, and not Helen's capacity, is what's slowing things down.

The fix is clear. And now, so is the path forward.

What happened?

In Scenario 1, the team operated in a typical "status quo" mode of collaboration—no principles, no structure, and no safety. Assumptions went unchecked, Helen didn't feel safe enough to speak up, and no real insight emerged. The result? Minimal changes and a growing problem that ultimately led to Helen's departure.

Scenario 2 was marginally better. Russ did "just say it" by naming the elephant in the room, but because Principles 1 (*Make the Abstract Clear*) and 2 (*Stop Assuming*) hadn't been established, the comment caused harm. His well-intentioned remark carried assumptions about Helen's age and capacity, leading to emotional fallout and permanent strain. The process got a short-term fix—but at the cost of trust.

Scenario 3 shows what's possible when all three principles are at play. Russ, acting as a facilitator, set the tone with ground rules (Principle 2), opened with a simple joy prompt to create connection, and then used sticky notes to make the team's process visible (Principle 1). That act of mapping turned something vague and ambiguous into something tangible and actionable.

But the real magic happened when Russ enacted Principle 3: *Just Say It.*

When Helen shared her vulnerability by sharing, "I feel like everyone thinks it's my fault," Russ didn't minimize it or try to steer past it. He demonstrated empathy by restating her words and naming the emotion. It might have seemed obvious, but in doing so, he normalized the presence of emotion in a professional setting. He modeled that feelings are not a liability in collaboration...they're data. And naming them creates space for healing, understanding, and forward movement. Russ' establishment of psychological safety invited the team to show up vulnerably and enact a real solution.

This is cue calling in action: noticing what's unspoken and

bringing it into the room with care.

Russ also handed over power—literally and figuratively—by giving Helen the sticky notes and inviting her to lead. In doing so, he signaled respect for her expertise and helped shift the conversation from blame to insight.

Then came the final unlock: once the process was visualized, the team realized that the bottleneck wasn't Helen; no, it was the three required approvals for each order. What looked like a "people problem" turned out to be a system issue.

When we make the abstract visible, stop assuming, and create the safety for people to just say it, collaboration gets real. And solutions become possible.

TIM'S STORY

One of the things we love most as facilitators is *cue calling*. It's a technique that took us time (and some brave improv classes!) to develop. In fact, it wasn't until we took a Meisner masterclass with the incredible improv/acting coach Johnny Kalida that we truly leaned into this skill and recognized it as a superpower.

Cue calling is simply this: naming what you see. It's noticing behaviors, body language, tone, and energy... and then bringing those cues into the room. It's calling out elephants. It's surfacing tension. It's saying, "something shifted," even if no one has named it yet.

With Tim's team, we did this a lot.

From the very first session, we called out what was obvious to us but unspoken in the room.

We cue called the team makeup: "It looks like we've got ten engineers; five who've been here a long time and five who are newer. That mix brings both history and fresh perspective."

We named our own position: "We don't have a history with this team or product, so we may ask some naive questions. Please bear with us, we're here to learn."

Throughout the session, we noticed and named whatever was surfacing:

When Jessica and Marcus connected over their mutual love of walking their dogs, we said, "Looks like we've got a shared joy in daily dog walks, that's a fun connection!"

When the room laughed at Tim's story about scaring his wife, we smiled and cue called, "Sounds like Tim's got a mischief streak the rest of you might not have known about."

When someone crossed their arms in response to a prompt, we gently said, "Lisa, I noticed you crossed your arms, which seems like something didn't land. What's coming up for you?"

When focus waned after an intense cluster-mapping session, we named it: "Looks like we might all need a break after that brain sprint. How about ten minutes?"

When Tim launched into a fast-paced verbal reflection, we stepped in: "Tim, you're connecting a lot of dots here, love that! Would you be open to jotting those down on sticky notes so we can capture them? And while he does that, does anyone else want to share what they're seeing?"

Over time, the group began to pick up the habit.

Marcus hesitated to speak, and Jessica jumped in: "Marcus, it looked like you had something to say—want to share it?"

After a well-received idea, Tim noted, "Seems like this one's lighting people up. Maybe it's a micro idea we can prototype?"

When a concept poster sparked excitement but misaligned with the group's target audience, someone spoke up: "This feels like a great solution, but maybe for a different audience than the one we've prioritized. What do you think?"

That moment led to a breakthrough. The group agreed that while the solution was strong, it didn't serve the current goal and decided to shelve it for future exploration.

By the end of our engagement, this team had learned to cue call for themselves. They had developed the muscle to notice, to name, and to navigate tension without triggering defensiveness or blame. They weren't just collaborating better; they were *seeing* better.

And all because they learned to *just say it*.

Summary of Principle 3: Just Say It

Let's review what we've learned about this third principle. In many instances, jumping to Principle 3 (*Just Say It*) without first building on Principles 1 (*Make the Abstract Clear*) and 2 (*Stop Assuming*) may exaggerate existing harmful conditions. These earlier steps create the foundation of clarity and trust that allows people to speak honestly without causing harm.

"Just Say It" is the embodiment of psychological safety, trust, and vulnerability. When the groundwork has been laid (i.e. via Principle 1 and Principle 2), people feel safe enough to express emotions, opinions, and even the ways a process or interaction may have caused harm or discomfort.

 **Let's be clear:** "Just Say It" is *not* a license to be unkind. It doesn't mean blurting out blunt criticisms or weaponizing honesty. Rather, it means welcoming emotion into the room, naming what's present, and normalizing open expression, without blame or judgment.

A facilitator can help others practice this principle using two key tools:

- **Reflecting/Reframing/Mirroring**
  This means repeating back what someone has said (using their language or slightly reframing it) to confirm you understand and to ensure the group heard it clearly. A simple way to start: "What I'm hearing you say is..."

- **Cue Calling**
  This means noticing nonverbal communication (things like tone, body language, energy shifts) and naming it out loud in a neutral way: "Your arms are crossed." "You got

quiet." "You seem frustrated." "I'm sensing some sadness." You're not labeling or diagnosing; rather, you're simply acknowledging what's showing up in the room.

At its best, *Just Say It* is an invitation.

It tells people: "Your voice matters here."

When one person is brave enough to speak their truth, it makes space for others to speak theirs, too.

Slow down to Speed Up

Principle 4 (*Slow Down to Speed Up*) is more than a tactic; it's a mindset. A philosophy. One that should thread through all the other principles we've discussed.

In our fast-paced work culture, it's easy for teams to race toward an expected outcome: a shiny new idea, an implementation plan, a revised product, a workaround for a barrier. Whatever the "end goal" might be, we're often pressured to get from Point A to Point Z as quickly as possible.

But collaboration doesn't work that way.

Humans are not machines; we're social creatures. Collaboration, at its core, is a human endeavor.

We can't bypass trust, shared understanding, and emotional alignment and still expect high-quality outcomes. Investing time early on in relationships, clarity, and process ensures we actually move *faster* and more effectively down the line. This is what the first three principles have already taught us.

But slowing down isn't just about group dynamics. It's essential for the creative and problem-solving process itself.

Einstein famously said, "If I had an hour to solve a problem, I'd spend 55 minutes thinking about the problem and 5 minutes thinking about solutions."

Modern research supports this. Studies in group creativity

show that truly novel, boundary-breaking ideas require *incubation,* or mental breathing room. The most creative insights rarely happen under pressure in a conference room. They show up in the shower, on a walk, in the garden, while stirring a pot of soup or drifting off to sleep.

Yet time and again, we ask teams to force brilliance on a schedule.

It's not just time that helps; diversity matters too. One well-known study compared the solution of a world-renowned subject matter expert with that of a randomly selected group of people (children included), who were pulled off the street and asked to solve the same problem. The results? A panel of judges found the group's ideas to be *more creative, more relevant,* and *more actionable* than those of the expert[33].

The takeaway: Effective problem-solving requires deliberate process and a mix of diverse people. This kind of collaboration takes time.

So, what does *Slow Down to Speed Up* actually look like in practice?

Beyond the basics (things like introductions, ground rules, relationship-building) it looks like this:
Resist the urge to jump into idea generation. Instead, take the time to **deeply understand the issue or opportunity at hand**. Name it. Break it down. Examine it from multiple angles. Only then should a group move into solution mode.

To bring this principle to life, let's share a story of a team that embraced it fully.

 *See It in Action*

A group of college mental health counselors wanted to better support first-time students living on campus. While the stigma around mental health has decreased significantly in recent years, and more college students are seeking help than ever before, many students still struggle. Loneliness, homesickness, and difficulty finding a sense of belonging continue to cause students to drop out after their first semester or fail to return for their second.

The counselors knew the problem existed, especially for first-generation college students who often lack the guidance or support to navigate the transition. This group of counselors were eager to brainstorm new ways to help; but first, they wanted to deeply understand what students are actually experiencing.

So, they invited some of their student workers to a collaboration session and encouraged them to bring a few friends along.

After reviewing ground rules and giving everyone a chance to introduce themselves, one of the lead counselors, Erin, kicked things off by asking the students to share some of the challenges they faced during their transition to college.

The conversation stalled.

The students hesitated, their answers brief and tentative. Erin tried rephrasing questions, encouraging participation...but the Q&A format wasn't landing. The energy in the room felt deflated. That's when Erin made a pivot.

She handed out sticky notes and asked everyone to think back to their first semester of college and write down memorable moments and the emotions they felt during those moments.

That changed everything.

Soon, everyone was writing feverishly. Sticky notes piled up. Erin drew a horizontal line across the whiteboard and invited everyone to come up and place their notes in chronological order.

The result was a shared "timeline of emotion." As more notes went up, clusters began to form: shared fears, common worries, recurring themes.

One big insight quickly emerged: many of the most significant emotions (which included things like fear of the unknown, worry about expectations, grief over leaving old friends, hope about starting fresh) started long *before* students ever arrived on campus.

One counselor stepped back and observed, "You know, the first time students hear about our mental health services is at orientation. But by then, they're overwhelmed with information. No wonder it doesn't stick."

The group had uncovered something they hadn't seen before: a missed opportunity to reach students earlier.

With this insight in hand, they worked alongside the students to design an information campaign that would launch as soon as students were admitted, instead of months later, when it was already too late.

Looking back, Erin later reflected, "If we hadn't brought the students in, and if we hadn't mapped out that timeline, we never would've seen it."

What happened?

Erin and her team practiced the first three principles: *Make the Abstract Clear, Stop Assuming,* and *Just Say It.* But they also embodied something deeper: the mindset behind Principle 4: *Slow Down to Speed Up.*

They started their collaboration well before anyone entered the room. Instead of jumping straight into brainstorming (which, let's be honest, would have been quicker and easier), they paused.

Erin and her colleagues realized that to create meaningful solutions, they needed student voices in the room. It would have been easy to skip that step. After all, they're the professionals—they talk with students every day. What could possibly be shared in that session that they hadn't already heard?

Turns out: a lot.

It took time to reach out, invite participation, and build trust with the students who joined. But without those voices, they would have been designing in a vacuum and solving for a problem without input from the people actually experiencing it.

Once the session began, the slow-down continued. The timeline exercise wasn't flashy. It took patience.

There were awkward silences, and probably a few participants quietly wondered, *Can't we just skip to solutions already?*

But by investing the time to understand the full emotional journey of a student's first experience with college (and by surfacing those emotions visually through practicing Principle 1: *Make the Abstract Concrete*), they unlocked a breakthrough.

They spotted a key leverage point that had been right in front of them all along: the moments *before* a student even arrives on campus.

That insight never would have emerged if they had rushed to action.

By slowing down, they were able to see more clearly. And by seeing clearly, they were able to speed up where it mattered most: developing targeted, meaningful, student-informed solutions.

TIM'S STORY

One of the ways we introduced this principle of *slowing down to speed up* with Tim's team was by asking them to sit in the *trouble* a little longer, and specifically, the trouble with their product.

We knew they would be eager to jump straight into solution mode. We as humans love to solve problems! They would naturally want to prototype, to build, and to move forward. But the truth was, they hadn't yet clearly defined what problems they were trying to solve, or why those problems mattered.

So, we paused them.

We told them that before they could move forward, they had to spend real time understanding the trouble. The collective groan in the room was...loud. And fair. They had already been sitting in this mess for weeks. They just wanted momentum.

So, we called it out.

"It sounds like you might not be excited about what we're asking you to do, and that's totally understandable," we said. "You've been in this space for a while, and you're ready to move. We get it. But we're asking you to trust the process, and right now, that process means slowing down. Like we experienced looking at the piece of art, remember?"

First, we asked them to interview ten external tech executives who had no ties to their organization. The team asked open-ended questions about the future of tech, including things like trends they were seeing, signals of change, evolving customer needs, upcoming legislation, and more. Within a week, the interviews were complete. Every comment, quote, and insight went onto digital sticky notes in a shared digital sticky note board.

Next, we challenged them to engage directly with their customers. They created a simple, interactive survey and sent it out. In just one week, they heard back from 50 customers. Those responses were also turned into sticky notes.

Then we brought them together for a two-hour synthesis session. They scanned, grouped, and labeled patterns in the data. Sticky notes began to cluster. Titles emerged. And then it happened:

An "aha" moment.

Amid the noise, three core problems stood out. Not ten. Not twenty. Just three. The moment they saw those, their posture shifted. What once felt like a swirl of overwhelm suddenly became actionable.

By slowing down—by gathering the diverse voices of people directly impacted by the work or product and resisting the urge to jump to solutions—they had finally arrived at clarity. And now, they could speed up with purpose, confidence, and shared alignment about what truly mattered.

Summary of Principle 4: Slow Down to Speed Up

Let's review what we've learned about this fourth principle.

Include the people you're designing for in the collaboration process.

This isn't always easy. Sometimes it's not even feasible, due to budget, timelines, or access. But when it is possible, centering the humans you're designing for can unlock insights you'd never find on your own. Their perspectives can surface needs, challenges, or missed opportunities that completely shift the direction (and success) of your work.

Take time to fully understand the topic before jumping to solutions.

We cannot overstate this. Before you brainstorm, make sure everyone is actually on the same page about the problem. Use tools like:

- A who, what, when, where, why, how prompt set
- A process map
- A timeline of emotions
- Or any visual framework that helps unpack the complexity

Doing this serves multiple purposes:

- It surfaces the *collective wisdom* of the group by inviting everyone's knowledge and perspective.

- It naturally encourages *grouping and clustering,* which accelerates understanding and cuts down on premature judgments (our brains love categories!).

- It helps *patterns emerge,* making your eventual

brainstorming much more focused, insightful, and grounded in reality.

- Most importantly, it increases your chances of identifying *true root causes*, instead of solving only for surface-level symptoms.

Slow down with intention to speed up with clarity.

Taking time to build shared understanding, both of the people and the problem, doesn't slow your team down. It sets the stage for deeper insight, better ideas, and stronger outcomes.

 ### *Walk Away with Something Actionable*

Nothing binds a group together like good collaboration. Working together to solve a challenge or generate new ideas can create a powerful sense of momentum, connection, and shared capability. When collaboration goes well, people leave feeling optimistic and energized by the belief that *together,* they can make things better.

But what happens *after* the collaboration can make or break that energy.

Do you know where hope goes to die in group collaboration? Inaction.

Cary found in her dissertation research that repeated cycles of collaboration followed by *no follow-through* don't just cause excitement to fizzle out—they actively harm people's trust in the process. Over time, those cycles lead to jadedness, cynicism, and even apathy[34].

Picture this: A group comes together to tackle a persistent problem. They co-create a solution that fits the need, stays within budget, and could be implemented immediately. The team is ecstatic. People are high-fiving. There's laughter, hope, even a few

"I'm so glad we finally did this!" comments.

And then...life happens.

People go back to the busyness of their day jobs. The brilliant solution fades into the background. It's mentioned once or twice in meetings, but other priorities take over. A year passes. At the next annual retreat, guess what's at the top of the agenda?

The exact same problem.

By this point, at least one or two team members are rolling their eyes. Someone says, "We tried this already," or, "What's the point? It's just going to die on the vine again." Even worse, people start attaching meaning to the inaction—making statements like, "Maybe the organization doesn't really *want* to change," or worse, "Maybe nothing actually *can* change."

Sound familiar?

When no meaningful progress is made, community erodes. Trust fades. And the void gets filled with skepticism, jadedness, and resistance[35]. That's the bad news.

The good news? "Meaningful progress" doesn't have to be huge.

You don't have to complete the whole project or reach the finish line. You just need *clear, visible steps* that move the group forward and to make sure people know those steps happened.

If no one knows about it, it's not meaningful.

What does meaningful progress look like?

If you love a good checklist, this one's for you: **Embed "Natural Next Steps" into every collaboration.** At the end of each session, don't let the room leave without asking, **"What are the natural next steps?"**

This question can anchor the transition from conversation to action. You don't need an elaborate project plan or fancy software (unless you want one). The tool you use doesn't matter (it could be a Kanban board, sticky notes, Trello, Monday.com, or just a shared Google Doc), but what matters is clarity and ownership.

Here's a simple template you can use that's embedded within

an example of what a completed "natural next steps" table might look like. Remember, it's not about capturing every detail to the nth degree or laying out a Work Breakout Structure in a Gantt chart. Just capture enough detail to keep things moving forward.

NEXT STEP	OWNER	TIMELINE	CHECK-IN POINT
Define what ___ means for our group	Taylor	End of week	Share draft at Monday check-in
Schedule customer interviews	Priya	Within 2 weeks	Report out in 2 weeks
Draft communication about ____	Alex	By Friday	Review in shared doc

 *Pro Tip: Don't assume the "leader" owns progress*

A common trap is assuming that the team leader or manager should be the one tracking progress and pushing follow-through. Why is this a trap? First, it equates title with accountability. The team leader does not need to be the one who owns every task. Second, because operational goals often take precedence for formal leaders. After all, they are held accountable by their bosses for team outcomes; their focus has to be on ensuring the team is hitting its operational targets. That means the important, strategic collaboration work can get quietly sidelined.

So instead of just assuming the leader owns progress

(remember Principle 2? *Stop assuming!*), try this: Assign an "Activator."

This person is selected by the group to help keep an eye on next steps, follow up with teammates, and nudge the group when energy dips. They're not in charge; rather, they're helping everyone stay in motion.

Think of the Activator as the collaboration's accountability buddy.

Communicate, even if the message is "no progress yet"

As Aristotle said, "Nature abhors a vacuum." So do people.

In the absence of information, our brains *fill in the gaps*. It's automatic and often unconscious—we draw from past experiences, rumors, or assumptions to explain what we don't know. Unfortunately, thanks to what psychologists call *negativity bias*, we tend to fill those gaps with the worst possible scenarios.

It gets worse: research shows that uncertainty is one of the biggest drivers of stress and anxiety[36]. When we don't hear anything, especially about something we were excited or emotionally invested in, we assume the worst.

The takeaway? "No news" is definitely *not* good news.

It might feel counterproductive, or even embarrassing, to send an update that says, "No progress yet." But in collaborative work, transparency and frequency of communication are critical.

Even if there's no forward movement, sharing status updates keeps people engaged. It reminds them of their excitement, validates their investment, and keeps the momentum from dying.

If you're the designated Activator, one of your most powerful tools is a simple check-in. Touch base with group members and communicate with the whole group regularly—*even if nothing major has happened yet*. A little communication goes a long way in maintaining trust and clarity.

 *Quick reminder: this works everywhere*

While this checklist of habits may feel most natural for established teams, these three simple practices apply to almost *any* collaborative group:

- **Define the natural next steps** at the end of every session

- **Assign an Activator** (or co-Activators) from within the group to track and nudge forward movement

- Communicate progress—or lack of it—clearly and regularly with the group

Whether you're:

- A **consortium of companies** trying to influence legislation

- A **Girl Scout troop** organizing for cookie season

- A group of **high school students** working on a final project

- A team of employees redesigning a frustrating process

- Or **faculty members** developing a brand-new degree program...

The collaboration doesn't end when the meeting ends.

Real collaboration lives in the **in-between spaces**—the actions, decisions, nudges, and communications that follow.

By embedding this principle of follow-through, you reinforce trust, reduce anxiety, and keep the collaboration alive and moving forward.

TIM'S STORY

Every week, we met with Tim's team for a two-hour session. At the start of each one, we let them know what we'd be doing and where we hoped to be by the end. Then, during the final 10 minutes, we carved out space for reflection: What did we accomplish? What themes emerged? What happened next?

Most of the next steps belonged to us, such as what we needed to do before the next session and what they could expect. But occasionally, the group had homework. For example, when we asked them to interview 10 external tech executives and survey 50 customers, we didn't just assign tasks, we co-designed them with the group.

Together, we outlined:

- What the next steps would look like
- Who would do them
- When they'd be done
- How we'd know they were complete

By staying true to Principles 1 and 2, we documented everything using sticky notes on the digital board and followed up with a summary email, so expectations were visible and clear.

The executive interviews:
Four team members volunteered. We noted their names, the process they designed, their agreed timeline (1-2 weeks, depending on availability), and the success criteria:

comments would be captured and shared in the digital board.

The customer survey:
Two team members took the lead. They outlined the plan: create the survey, compile a customer email list, craft and send the message, track responses, and post feedback on the digital board. Again, we tracked who was responsible, what the process looked like, when it would be done (within a week), and how we'd measure completion.

Every time we asked the group to do something between sessions, we made sure they had a clear understanding of the what, who, when, and why, and we made the schedule visible to everyone.

Were there times when something didn't get done? Of course. Life happens. But when it didn't happen, it wasn't because people didn't know what to do. It was because of real constraints like emergencies, competing priorities, or new information. And because the expectations were clear, it didn't break trust. It helped build it.

Clear, shared expectations gave the group a sense of calm. They knew what was coming. They had space to follow through. And with each small step completed, their trust in each other and in the process grew.

By the end of our engagement, they didn't need us to document next steps anymore. They were doing it themselves. More importantly, Tim, as the project leader, had made it part of his regular practice.

Summary of Principle 5: Walk away with something actionable

Let's recap what we've learned about this fifth principle.

High-stakes collaboration is rarely "one and done." It almost always requires sustained effort after the meeting, session, or workshop ends.

If there's no clear path forward, the energy and community built during collaboration can quickly unravel. When momentum stalls, it opens the door to frustration, jadedness, anxiety, and even apathy.

On the flip side, **meaningful progress** helps maintain optimism and trust, while also keeping the group moving forward.

But here's the good news: meaningful progress doesn't have to be big. It just has to be:

Even a small step forward matters, especially when everyone knows it's happening.

To embed this principle into your collaboration process, remember these three simple actions:

1. **Document the Natural Next Steps.**
   Define what needs to happen, who's responsible, by when, and what success looks like.

2. **Designate an Activator.**
   This is the person (not necessarily the team lead!) who checks in on the tasks and keeps momentum going.

3. **Communicate often and transparently.**
   Even if the update is, "Nothing has happened yet," say it.
   Transparency builds trust; silence breeds doubt.

When a group walks away with clarity on next steps and a process for staying accountable, they don't just leave the meeting.
They leave aligned, empowered, and ready to act.

Principle
6

Plan to Pivot

At first glance, this principle might seem like a contradiction to everything we've said so far. But don't worry, we're not abandoning structure. In fact, we're reinforcing its purpose.

We've talked a lot about the importance of structure in high-stakes collaboration, and in the next chapter, we'll share some ways you can incorporate it into practice for yourself. But we want to take this moment to emphasize the idea that having a collaboration process doesn't mean clinging to it no matter what. A good collaboration design must bend with the group's needs, not break them.

You've probably experienced the opposite: a meeting with a strict agenda where a meaningful, productive conversation was suddenly cut short because it "wasn't on the agenda." Cue the dreaded phrases like, "Let's not get off topic," or "We need to stick to the schedule."

Now, we're not saying group conversations should be allowed to wander aimlessly into cat stories or houseplant survival tips. But sometimes, what a group *really* needs to talk about isn't what's written on the agenda.

Here's the thing: when a team follows the first five principles of collaboration, they often uncover something unexpected— something that was literally unseeable or unknowable at the start. When this happens, the plan must shift.

Let's look at an example:

Remember the purchasing policy story scenarios with Russ and Helen? The team thought they were meeting to revise wording in the existing purchasing policy document. But once they began applying Principle 1 (*Make the Abstract Clear*), they visualized the current purchasing process with sticky notes and realized the root cause of their issue wasn't the policy at all. It was the requirement for too many approvals. That "aha" moment could only happen because the team pivoted away from the agenda and toward what the group *really* needed to explore.

Or think about Principle 4 (*Slow Down to Speed Up*). Sometimes slowing down reveals that you need a completely different set of stakeholders in the room. Bringing them in might require a whole new process, timeline, or budget. But skipping that step risks designing a solution that doesn't actually serve its intended audience.

Here's the truth: *something* will happen in your collaboration that you didn't plan for. That's not a failure of your process. That's the beauty of it.

In fact, if you're doing high-stakes collaboration right (and if you're practicing the first five principles) then you *should* expect the unexpected. New insights will emerge. People will say things that shift the direction of the work. Unspoken tensions will surface. Undervalued opportunities will come to light.

That's not a derailment. That's progress.

The Plan to Pivot Mindset

A strong collaboration process is less like a railroad track and more like Google Maps.

Let's say you're driving to an important meeting at a place you've never been. You're a planner. You love being on time. Lucky for you, your colleague Jenn sends you a step-by-step set of directions. You've got this.

You're cruising along, music playing, plenty of time to spare.

And then brake lights, a sea of them: traffic is at a dead stop.

The radio announcer says there's been a major accident on your route. You have a choice:

In the days before GPS, you'd either sit there and be late... or you'd exit and try to wing it.

But now, Google Maps shows you two alternate routes that will get you where you need to go.

You pivot. You arrive. You're still on time.

Changing the navigation process didn't change the *destination*. It gave you new ways to get there.

That's what planning to pivot looks like.

And if you're someone who struggles to let go of structure, who finds ambiguity uncomfortable, we have a recommendation for you: take an improv class. Seriously!

Improv teaches you how to embrace uncertainty, listen deeply, adapt on the fly, and respond to the moment. It's one of the most powerful tools we've used to become more flexible facilitators.

Because in high-stakes collaboration, your job isn't just to follow a plan. Your job is to respond to what the group needs *now*, even if it's not what you originally anticipated.

Plan thoughtfully. Design carefully. And be ready to pivot.

The Art of Adaptability: Improvisation

If the phrase "make it up as you go" makes you start to sweat, we again suggest taking an improv class.

In *The Improv Mindset*, Bruce and Gail Montgomery define improvisation as "the act of spontaneous creation"—in other words, making something out of nothing[37]. That might sound chaotic, but in practice, good improv is anything but. It's structured, connected, and surprisingly clarifying.

As we've shared, most of us grew up learning the rules of teamwork through sports or school projects: know your role, follow the leader, stick to the playbook. Improv flips that. In improv, whether it's jazz, dance, or acting, there are no fixed roles.

Leadership shifts moment to moment. The only thing everyone follows is a set of foundational principles. And when those are followed, magic happens.

Failure is expected. In fact, not only is it expected, but it's also often hilarious.

When everyone's tuned into each other and adjusting, responding, and building, it creates a shared rhythm that feels euphoric. People walk away saying, "Wow, that felt so good."

If you've never seen or done improv, it can feel hard to picture. So, let's walk you through it.

The Improv Mindset in Action

As Bruce and Gail Montgomery outline in their book, improv is grounded in four key principles:

1. Yes, and...
2. Listen with the intent to serve
3. Support your teammates at all costs
4. Trust your instincts

Imagine you're in a group of six people, all familiar with these principles. You get a prompt: *herding cats.*

Your first thought? *Ugh, cliché, and impossible.* But you honor the principle of *Yes, and...,* so the game begins.

Larry steps in as a cat farmer in Nebraska, calling his cats back to the barn. You decide to support the world he's building by jumping in as a cat. But not just any cat; no, you're a talking, distinguished cat with a very posh British accent.

You say, "My dear Larry, must we do this all day? I've grown weary of this routine."

Someone else jumps in as another refined feline: "Yes, Larry, we were bred for finer things, not the pastures of Wyoming."

You gently correct, "Cornelius, we're in Nebraska."

"Oh yes, silly me," the cat replies. "I was never any good at geography in cat school." You both burst into a ridiculous, high-society laugh.

That slip—a mistake about the location—could have derailed the scene. But in improv, mistakes are part of the fun. They're acknowledged, folded in, and used to move the story forward.

Larry could have shut things down and steered the scene back to "realistic" cat herding. But instead, he adapts.

"Oh goodness," he says, "talking cats! Well, this changes everything!"

The scene escalates beautifully. Suddenly, Larry is conducting a cat choir for the Queen of Scotland, and the cats are wearing top hats.

What just happened?

- Everyone contributed.
- Roles and power shifted fluidly.
- They trusted their instincts.
- They embraced their mistakes.
- They pivoted with ease—and joy.

So...What Does This Have to Do with Collaboration?

Everything.

Improv teaches us to let go of rigid control, respond to what's unfolding, and trust in the moment. In high-stakes collaboration, adaptability isn't a bonus; it's essential. That's the heart of Principle 6: *Plan to Pivot.*

If you want to get better at collaboration, practicing improv is one of the fastest ways to build the muscles you need. Listening, trust, adaptability, and collective momentum are all things great collaborators bring to the table.

But don't worry: you don't *have* to take an improv class to practice this principle. You can embrace the improv mindset by keeping a few things in mind:

Practicing the Pivot

In high-stakes collaboration, the design you start with (i.e. the structure, activities, timing) *will* need to change.

Let's say that again for the folks in the back: *It. Will. Change.*

So rather than letting it be a thing of uncertainty and fear, plan for change. Here's how:

- **Anticipate derailments.** Look at your design and ask, "Where might things go sideways? What if a conversation takes longer than expected?" Build backup plans.

- **Co-design with your partner from the group.** Ask, "Where might tension show up? Where do you think emotions might get high?" Build in cushions for the unexpected.

- **Buffer your time.** If you have four hours, design for three and a half. Don't schedule down to the minute—leave space to breathe.

- **When you pivot, *name it*.** Draw on Principle 3: *Just Say It.* If you sense the group is lost or needs something else, say so. "Team, I know we planned to move into design, but I'm hearing that we're not quite aligned on the current process. What if we slow down here until we're ready to move on?" Saying it out loud builds trust, diffuses uncertainty, and models the very behaviors you're asking the group to adopt. It's Principle 2 (*Stop Assuming*) and Principle 3 (*Just Say It*) in action.

TIM'S STORY

Working with Tim's team, we had to pivot a *lot*. Almost every session required some kind of real-time adjustment.

Sometimes they needed more time on an activity than we'd planned. We'd feel the momentum building and realize: they're not done yet. So, we shifted by adjusting the timing of what came next, or cutting a later piece altogether and saving it for the following session.

Other times, they breezed through something we expected would take a while. When that happened, we filled the extra time with something relational: a short improv game, a quick moment of storytelling, or a prompt like, *Tell us about a time you failed miserably at something.* These activities weren't just "filler"; they built connection and trust.

One moment stands out clearly.

Midway through a session, we were transitioning into small group breakouts when Jessica raised her hand. "Actually," she said, "instead of splitting up, could we stay as one group for this? I think it would be a richer discussion and I really want to hear what everyone thinks."

Now, *that* was not part of our plan.

We'd designed the whole session around breakout groups. All our materials and facilitation notes were tailored to small group dynamics. But as Jessica spoke, we saw heads nodding across the room. The group clearly wanted this.

So, we said, "Sure, we can do that. Let's take a five-minute break while we reconfigure."

As the team stretched and grabbed coffee, we huddled

like mad scientists. Whispering and scribbling on the back of our notes, we pulled from our facilitation toolbox and rebuilt the structure on the fly. We reframed the exercise so it would work with the full group to maintain energy, keep everyone engaged, and still guide them toward the outcome we needed.

And it worked. Beautifully.

In fact, it worked *better* than our original plan. The conversation was deeper, more energized, and more unifying than it likely would have been in smaller groups. Jessica's instinct, and the group's response, showed us exactly what was needed.

We were so glad we listened. That pivot became a turning point in how they engaged, both with the content and with each other.

Summary of Principle 6: Plan to Pivot

Let's recap what we've learned about this sixth principle:

- **Nothing in high-stakes collaboration will go exactly as planned.** That's not a failure—it's a feature. Humans are complex, emotions are real, and collaboration reveals what was previously unseen.

- **The key is to anticipate where your design might need to flex** and have some backup options ready. Thinking through a few possible pivots in advance helps you stay grounded and confident in the moment.

- Want to build your flexibility muscle? **Take an improv class.** It's one of the fastest, most fun ways to strengthen your adaptability and response instincts.

- **When a pivot happens, don't just silently change course.** Use Principle 2 (*Stop Assuming*) and Principle 3 (*Just Say It*): let the group know what's shifting, why it's shifting, and what you're noticing that prompted the change. Reflect back what you're seeing to model transparency and responsiveness.

- Because ultimately, failing to plan for change is planning to fail. (Thanks, Ben Franklin.)

Plan to pivot—because something will change. And if you're ready, that change can unlock even better outcomes than what you imagined.

So...What Now?

You don't need to memorize all six principles or master every tool overnight.

The point is: when collaboration feels messy or hard, or when you're unsure what's going wrong, you now have a way to diagnose what might be missing. These principles are your scaffolding. They don't guarantee perfection, but they give you something solid to stand on when things feel uncertain.

Collaboration isn't just a meeting or a moment—**it's a practice.**

It's built in the small choices you make:

- Pausing to clarify an idea
- Setting expectations
- Acknowledging emotion
- Slowing down the rush to solve
- Taking one next step forward
- Being open to change when it comes

The more you use these principles, the more intuitive they'll become. Eventually, you'll start noticing when a group needs one, and how you might gently offer it. You don't need a fancy title or a room full of sticky notes to be the person who says, "Hey, before we keep going, can we make sure we're all talking about the same thing?"

So...What's Next?

In the next chapter, we'll take everything you've learned and walk you through the **design process behind effective collaboration sessions**. Think of the principles as your blueprint. Next, we'll demonstrate how to take these principles and turn them into sessions, meetings, and moments that move people forward.

Because now that you know the principles...Let's talk about the practice.

Chapter 5
Done!

Putting the Principles Into Motion

After Tim's first solo session, something else shifted. Not dramatically. Not with fireworks. But in the quiet, steady way a new habit forms, by taking one step at a time.

He didn't become a master facilitator overnight. But he kept showing up. He kept practicing. And most importantly, he kept using the principles.

Over the next few weeks, we continued working with Tim and the team. Only now, our role had changed. We weren't leading the sessions anymore; instead, we were designing *with* Tim behind the scenes, helping him sequence the work and anticipate the pivots. And each session became a kind of laboratory: a place to test how far the group had come, and where they still needed support.

During one week, they mapped out stakeholder priorities. They made the abstract clear by visualizing the tensions between customer needs, engineering feasibility, and long-term business goals.

Another week, they tackled their assumptions head-on. Tim prompted them with a now-familiar question: "What are we assuming here, and what might happen if we're wrong?"

In a later session, when a conversation turned tense, he

paused and said, "I'm hearing some strong opinions and a little frustration. That's okay. Let's take a breath, name what's surfacing, and work through it together."

They didn't always get it right. But each session built on the last. Every principle they practiced gave the next one a stronger foundation.

By the end of our engagement, the team had co-created:

Three validated design directions

A clear implementation roadmap

A system for capturing customer feedback and integrating it into product development

A new shared language for working together

But the biggest win wasn't any of those deliverables. It was this: they didn't need us anymore.

Tim was designing and guiding the sessions. The group was owning the process. They'd stopped waiting for permission to collaborate. They weren't just using the principles. They were living them.

CHAPTER 6
Putting It into Practice

From Learning to Leading

You've learned the six principles of high-stakes collaboration. You've seen them in action through Tim's story, felt the tension and triumph of applying them with a real team, and maybe even caught glimpses of your own team in the examples we shared.

But here's the thing: understanding the principles isn't the same as practicing them.

So how do you begin?

This chapter is your bridge between ideas and action. It's not about mastering every technique or facilitating full-scale collaboration sessions (though you might get there). It's about choosing one thing. One principle. One moment. And starting small.

We call this *everyday practice*: building your collaborative muscle through small, repeatable actions.

 ***If you feel overwhelmed, start with the principle that calls to you***

It may seem like we're contradicting ourselves here: as we mentioned in Chapter 5, the best course of action is to apply the principles in order. However, we also understand it may feel overwhelming to try and implement all six. And when we're overwhelmed and fight, flight, or freeze kicks in, we tend to avoid trying new things[38]. In the case of the principles, some momentum forward is better than no change at.

Start where the pain is. Start where the energy is. You don't need to start with all six. Choose one.

Maybe you're someone who loves clarity and gets frustrated when meetings feel like a foggy mess. Then Principle 1: *Make the Abstract Clear* might be your natural starting point.

Maybe you've watched your team tiptoe around hard truths or misinterpret each other's intentions. That's a good sign to try Principles 2 and 3: *Stop Assuming* and *Just Say It*. Sometimes, jumping to Principles 2 and 3 is as simple as saying "I'm going to be brave and say something that might need to be said...", and share with the team. By prefacing with a vulnerable statement, you're setting the groundwork for an open conversation.

Or maybe you're exhausted by whiplash decision-making and constant pivots. Principle 4: *Slow Down to Speed Up* could be your new mantra.

Reflection prompt:

- Which principle do you wish your team used more often?
- Which principle feels hardest for you to practice?
- Which one feels easiest?

 ***Choose a tiny experiment***

We don't need big plans. We need small, doable experiments.

Let's say you want to practice Principle 1: *Make the Abstract Clear.*

Your experiment could be as simple as saying, "Before we move on, can we write everything down that we are all saying on sticky notes so we can all see them?" And then do it—on a digital whiteboard, a shared doc, or just on the table in front of you.

If it's *Stop Assuming,* your experiment might sound like: "Just to make sure we're aligned, can we each share what we think we're trying to solve?"

If it's *Just Say It,* maybe you name what's not being said: "I'm sensing some tension here—am I the only one?"

None of these require permission. You don't have to be the leader or the facilitator. You just have to speak up, gently.

Try this:

- Think about your next meeting or group conversation.
- Choose one tiny behavior shift to try.
- Commit to practicing it once. Just once.

 ### *Reflect and adjust*

You don't need a fancy debrief. Just take 2 minutes after the interaction and ask yourself:

- Did I try the principle I committed to?
- How did it feel?
- How did the group respond?
- Would I do anything differently next time?

This isn't about perfection. It's about noticing. Because the more we notice, the more we learn to read the room, adapt our approach, and build confidence.

Note: You don't need a perfect outcome to count it as a success. The win is in the trying.

 *Invite others in*

Once you've practiced a principle a few times, it becomes easier to model it for others. You might even invite a colleague to join you:

- "I'm trying to practice clearer collaboration—do you want to experiment with this with me?"

- "Can we take 5 minutes to visualize this idea before we keep talking about it?"

- "Let's try identifying assumptions before we move forward, just for fun."

You don't need to make it a big professional development program or learning session. Remember, you're just building a different way of being together.

 *Give it time*

Collaboration is a habit. Not a heroic act.

You're not trying to be the savior of every meeting. You're just trying to plant small seeds through questions, prompts, and different ways of "showing up" in meetings, that make better collaboration more likely.

Over time, these small shifts create new norms. You'll start to notice people writing more things down, asking better questions, or even reflecting back unspoken feelings. And then, maybe event without realizing it, you'll have helped create a culture of collaboration.

One behavior at a time. One moment at a time.

 *Final Thought*

You don't need to be the Tim of your story...yet.

But you can be the person who helps someone else see something more clearly.

- You can be the one who names what others are afraid to say.

- You can pause when the rush to solve takes over, and say, "Let's slow down."

- You can be the one who remembers the path forward, and gently holds others to it.

This is what this work is.

This is what practicing these principles looks like.

And this is where real change begins.

Starting Strong

Almost a year had passed when the email arrived. It was from Tim. He had been promoted.

Subject line: Need your magic again (but this time, from the start).

After leading the redesign initiative to completion and earning not only internal accolades, but also witnessing a massive culture shift in how teams collaborated, he'd been tapped to lead a brand-new innovation team. The team included ten people from across the organization who had no history together. No baggage. No bruises. Just a clean slate and a bold challenge: build something new and build it fast.

"I don't want things to break down," Tim wrote. "I want to get this right from the beginning. I want to give this group what we didn't have when we started on my product team. Can we bring you in early to help us build the foundation?"

We scheduled a call the next day.

"I keep thinking about our early sessions," he told us. "All the misfires, the assumptions, the unspoken tension. If we had done more to get to know each other upfront—really understand how we each work and what we need—I think we could've moved faster and had less friction."

He paused.

"Anyway, I want this new team to start from connection. Not conflict."

We smiled. Because this was the dream. Not being brought in to fix something broken, but to form something strong from the very beginning.

The Workshop

Two weeks later, we kicked off a one-day session with Tim's new team.

Not a retreat. Not a training.

A forming workshop.

After a fun improv game to get the group warmed up, we dove into our first activity of the day with *About Me* postcards, which are a simple but powerful exercise that surfaces working styles and what people need in order to work well together. Each person filled in:

- Name and Role
- Working Style Sliders (Early Bird ↔ Night Owl, Introvert ↔ Extrovert, Ideator ↔ Executor...)
- Superpowers
- What I Struggle With
- What I Need to Collaborate
- How I Approach Conflict
- What Helps Me Feel Seen and Valued

One by one, they stood up and introduced themselves. There was laughter. A few surprising moments. One person confessed that they always need time to process before making decisions. Another shared that if they seem blunt, it's not because they don't care; it's just their default wiring. In the room, you could feel it click: *Oh. That's why you show up the way you do.*

From there, we mapped all the slider responses on a board and reflected on what the distribution revealed: patterns, quirks, strengths. We used that insight to co-create a *Ways of Working Agreement,* which is a living document that captured team norms, from when to schedule meetings to how decisions would get made.

Then we shifted into values. We guided the team through a modified Ikigai activity, helping them name what they love, what they're good at, and what they believe the world needs more of. Clustering their sticky notes, we uncovered shared values: curiosity, follow-through, equity, and play. And then we asked the key question: **"What does this value look like in action?"**

The result was a tangible set of behaviors the team could hold each other to; not just pretty words or posters for the wall, but a real-time compass.

Next, we led them through a **Conflict and Repair planning activity**, where they brainstormed, discussed, and documented how they'd navigate difficult moments. How would they speak up? How would they make amends? What did they want each other to do if (or, since they were being honest with each other, when) something went wrong?

Then came the laughter: the **Team Naming exercise**. After riffing on their shared traits (big dreams, chaotic whiteboards, a love of late-night thinking), they landed on a name that made everyone smile: The Midnight Architects.

Finally, we wrapped with a **Team Charter and Collaboration Rhythm**: a summary of their mission, the outcomes they were chasing, and how they'd communicate, meet, and track progress.

Afterward

As people packed up, Tim caught our eye.

"This felt like building the runway before trying to take off," he said. "Last year, we were trying to fly the plane while fixing the engine midair." He paused. "This time, it already feels different."

We nodded. "Because this time, you didn't assume collaboration would just happen. You designed for it."

He grinned. "Let's see where we can go from here!"

CHAPTER 7
Sustaining Long-Term Team Collaboration

In high-stakes, long-term collaboration, success isn't just about hitting deadlines or launching great ideas: it's about nurturing the human connections that make all of that possible. Teams aren't machines. They're dynamic, living systems. And just like any living thing, they need care, attention, and intentional design, especially at the beginning.

Too often, teams dive into "the work" without ever learning how to work together. It should be no surprise, then, when they hit barriers: mistrust, miscommunication, confusion about roles, or clashing styles. They never really formed. They just...got to work.

This chapter is your guide to the **Forming Phase**—the foundational stage that's most often skipped and most critical to team cohesion. We'll walk you through practical tools and activities we use to help teams build trust, understand one another, and align on how they'll collaborate before the real work begins.

The Lifecycle of a Team

Borrowing from Bruce Tuckman's 1965 team development model, teams progress through four stages:

1. **Forming**—Building relationships and setting expectations

2. **Storming**—Navigating disagreement and establishing roles

3. **Norming**—Solidifying patterns of communication and collaboration

4. **Performing**—Operating at a high-functioning level to achieve shared goals

Most teams, especially in high-stakes environments, try to jump straight to Performing—only to get stuck in the Storming phase. Why? Because they skipped Forming. Why did they skip Forming? It's all part of the *Collaboration Illusion* : we assume that because we're smart people who can communicate, we don't need all of the "fluffy stuff" and can just automatically work well together.

Hopefully, we've convinced by now that the "fluffy stuff" of collaboration is critical to performance.

And if you're ready to learn how to create high performing teams from the very beginning, rather than deal with the pain that comes from skipping the Forming stage, here's some simple tools we've found to be very effective.

Tools to Help Teams Form

When Tim reached out and asked us to support his new team, he wasn't just looking for a kick-off agenda or a few icebreakers. He wanted something more foundational; something that would set his team up to *collaborate well* from the very beginning.

Why? Because he'd lived through what happens when you don't.

He remembered what it felt like to be in a team where trust had eroded, assumptions had piled up, and people stopped talking altogether. He'd seen how hard it was to rebuild collaboration once it was broken. But more importantly, he'd experienced the shift that happens when a team is given the space, structure, and support to work *with* each other, not just alongside each other.

This time, he wanted to do it differently.

He wanted to invest in the *forming* phase.

And that's exactly what we helped him do.

We walked Tim's new team through a structured set of activities designed to help them get to know one another—not just as roles or titles, but as whole humans. We helped them talk openly about how they prefer to work, what they need from others to collaborate well, what they struggle with, and even how they handle conflict.

It wasn't about "team building" in the traditional sense. It was about *team designing*: co-creating a way of being together that would support honest dialogue, productive tension, and real progress over time.

The results?

This new team gelled faster, tackled complexity with more grace, and built trust that didn't need to be "fixed" later. They didn't just do the work. They became a team capable of doing *great* work together.

In the next section, we'll walk you through the exact tools and activities we used with Tim's team—and countless others—to encourage the forming phase. Whether you're kicking off a new project or re-starting with fresh intention, these practices will help your team lay a strong, resilient foundation for collaboration.

Let's dive in.

Forming Activity 1: Guide to Me

In the "Guide to Me" activity, we have each participant of this collaborative group answer some key questions that will help others better understand them. We create a postcard-like document with questions that we ask them to answer. Once they answer the questions, they each stand up and present their "Guide to Me" postcard to the whole group.

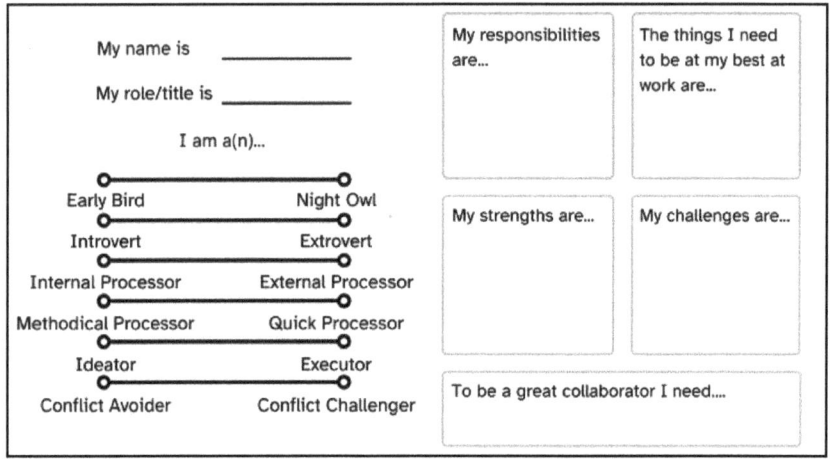

The questions are:

1. My name is....
2. My role/title is.....
3. I am a.....(these are dimensions that focus on working styles)

Early Bird ↔ Night Owl

Introvert ↔ Extrovert

Internal Processor ↔ External Processor

Methodical Processor ↔ Quick Processor

Ideator ↔ Executor

Conflict Avoider ↔ Conflict Challenger

For these, participants mark where they think they fit on the slider scale based on their most natural behavior. Sometimes, people will say things like…. *"I can be both an ideator and an executor depending on what is needed"* and that is okay. But the follow up question is: of the 2, which do you find yourself engaging in most? Or between the 2, which do you enjoy most?

4. My responsibilities (in my role or title) are…
5. The things I need to be at my best at work are…
6. My strengths (superpowers) are…
7. My challenges (areas I am looking to improve are) are…
8. To be a great collaborator I need…

Additional questions can be added to the "Guide to Me" postcard activity if the group thinks there are additional things that might be helpful to know about each other.

Once each participant has shared their "Guide to Me" postcards, ask all participants to mark their working style preferences on a collaborative board.

Being able to see as a group how everyone maps will make for a really rich discussion and discovery.

This will also allow the next activity to take place: "Ways of Working."

Forming Activity 2: Ways of Working

Once you've taken time to get to know each other as humans and surfaced your individual work style preferences, it's time to translate that insight into shared ground rules and team norms.

For example, if most people identify as early birds, consider scheduling key meetings or deep work blocks earlier in the day. On the other hand, if your group includes a mix of early birds and night owls, mid-day meetings might offer the best compromise.

Or take processing styles: if 10 out of 12 people are external processors and 2 are internal, it's important not to misinterpret silence. Those quieter participants aren't disengaged—they're thinking. So, you might build in intentional pauses or check-ins to make sure everyone's voice is heard before moving on.

Similarly, if most team members need time to reflect before making decisions, don't expect alignment in a single meeting. Instead, send information in advance, or dedicate one session to discussion and the next to decision-making. That extra time isn't a delay; it's an accelerator for quality outcomes and inclusive collaboration.

The key insight here is that **you never know what a team needs until you ask**. And even one new person can shift the dynamic. But something powerful happens when people see their differences surfaced visually and then talk about what those differences mean for how they want to work together.

Whatever themes emerge, use them to co-create a "Ways of Working" document: a clear, shared reference point for how your team will operate.

It doesn't have to be fancy—but it does need to be documented to help *Make the Abstract Clear*. Putting it in writing helps make the invisible visible, and it gives everyone something to return to when friction inevitably arises.

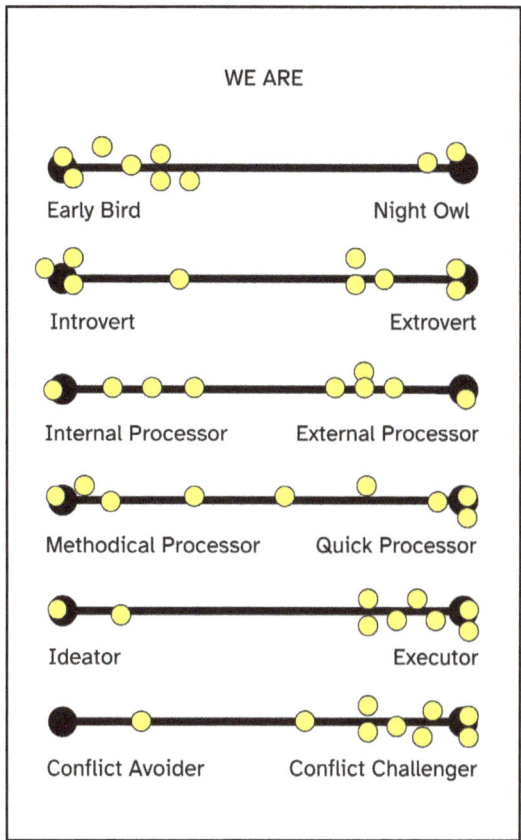

Early Birds vs. Night Owls

Example Agreement: We'll schedule core meetings between 10am—3pm to accommodate energy peaks across the team.

Introverts vs. Extroverts

Example Agreement: Make space for 1:1 or written follow-ups after group sessions for deeper thinking.

External vs. Internal Processors

Example Agreement: Give advance notice on key discussion topics so folks can process ahead of time.

Methodical Processors vs. Quick Processors

Example Agreement: Avoid immediate decision-making in high-stakes meetings and leave space to revisit after reflection.

Ideators vs. Executors

Example Agreement: Assign clear roles in meetings: some focus on idea generation, others on shaping them into actions.

Conflict Avoiders vs. Conflict Challengers

Example Agreement: Use structured formats (e.g., Start/Stop/Continue, Rose-Thorn-Bud) to surface tensions productively.

Forming Activity 3: Values in Action

Once the team has mapped their ways of working, we move into values, which articulates what matters most to each individual and, ultimately, to the group.

This step deepens connection. It invites participants to bond over the beliefs and motivations that shape their choices—not just how they work, but why they work the way they do.

We often use the **Ikigai Framework** to guide this activity. *Ikigai* is a Japanese concept that loosely translates to "reason for being." It invites reflection across four dimensions:

1. What you love
2. What you're good at
3. What the world needs more of
4. What you could be paid for (We sometimes skip this step when clients are already established in their role. It becomes especially valuable during career searches or transitions.)

Ikigai

What you love to do

What you are good at

What the world needs more of

★ EMERGING VALUES/PURPOSE

Step 1: What Matters to Me

For this values-focused activity, we concentrate on the first three. Question by question, we ask participants to reflect on the question, and write their answers on sticky notes (usually around 5—6 per question) in the corresponding circle in the framework:

- First, "What do you love to do?"
- Then, "What are you good at?"
- Finally, "What does the world need more of?"

Once they are done, we ask participants to bring their sticky notes and post them on a shared board (physical or digital) in their corresponding circles in the framework.

As a group, they then cluster responses into themes and look for patterns:

1. Where are the overlaps?
2. What shows up across the group?

What emerges is a visual map of personal purpose that quickly becomes shared purpose. Though each person brings their own perspective, most teams discover a powerful convergence.

For example, one group might notice that creativity, curiosity, and connection surface again and again. These become candidate **core values**.

Ikigai

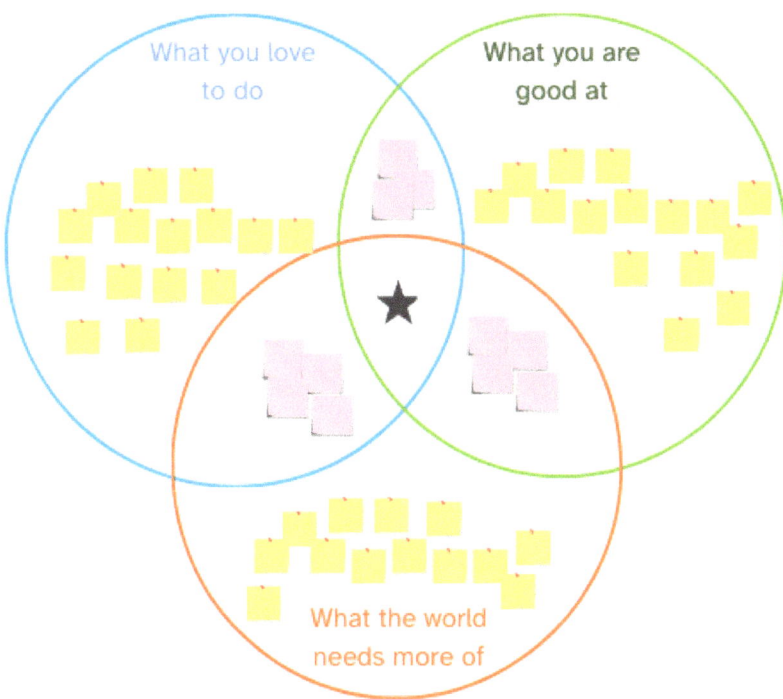

EMERGING VALUES/PURPOSE

1. Collaborating with Others
2. Innovating/Creating Solutions
3. Acting with Integrity
4. Empowering Others
5. Creating Inclusive and Welcoming Spaces
6. Sustainability
7. Curiosity/Always Wanting to Learn
8. Transparency
9. Generosity

Step 2: What Matters to Us

Once core values candidates are determined, teams take these values a step further: **What do these values look like in action?** For instance, if "curiosity" is an emerging value, what are the tangible behaviors that bring curiosity to life?

The group might say: asking open-ended questions, staying in "explore" mode before shifting into solution mode, or using "why" and "tell me more" as regular prompts.

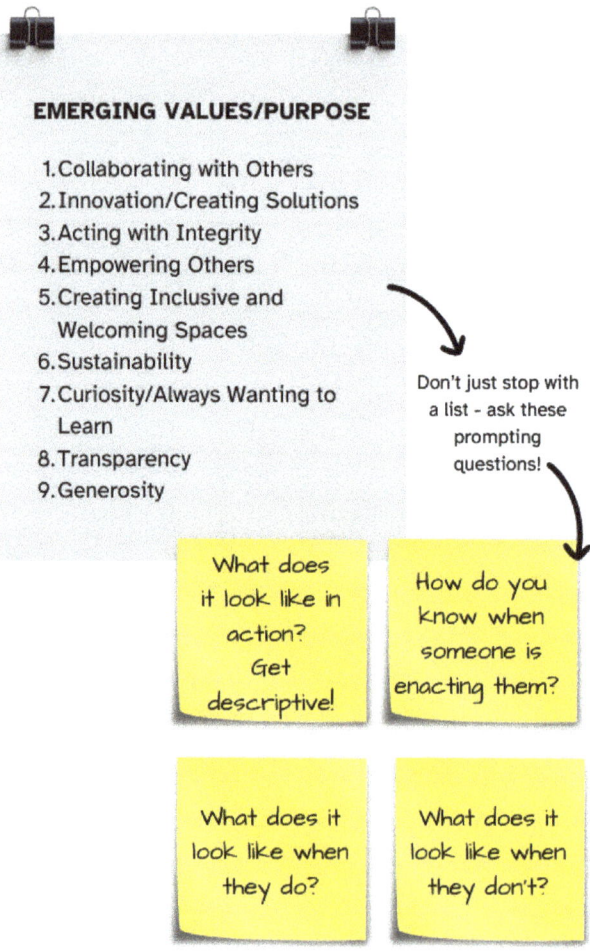

EMERGING VALUES/PURPOSE

1. Collaborating with Others
2. Innovation/Creating Solutions
3. Acting with Integrity
4. Empowering Others
5. Creating Inclusive and Welcoming Spaces
6. Sustainability
7. Curiosity/Always Wanting to Learn
8. Transparency
9. Generosity

Don't just stop with a list - ask these prompting questions!

What does it look like in action? Get descriptive!

How do you know when someone is enacting them?

What does it look like when they do?

What does it look like when they don't?

Step 3: How We'll Show Up

This final step, "translating values into observable behaviors", is essential. It shifts values from being abstract ideals into shared expectations the team can live by. And that sets the stage for deeper alignment, stronger trust, and a clear cultural foundation to guide the collaboration ahead.

Examples are:

- **Collaborating with Others:** Team members co-create a project plan together, openly share updates, and step in to support each other when deadlines shift.

- **Innovation/Creative solutions:** The team brainstorms new ways to serve clients, tests a pilot program, and refines it based on real feedback instead of sticking to old methods.

- **Acting with Integrity:** A team member admits an error in a client deliverable, corrects it quickly, and communicates transparently about what was done to fix it.

- **Empowering Others:** Team leads rotate facilitation roles so everyone has a chance to lead meetings and showcase their strengths.

- **Creating Inclusive and Welcoming Spaces:** During meetings, the team ensures everyone has time to speak and intentionally invites quieter voices into the discussion.

- **Sustainability:** The team implements a reusable materials system for events rather than using single-use items each time.

- **Curiosity/Always Wanting to Learn:** Team members regularly share "what we learned this week" at the end of meetings, sparking cross-learning and new ideas.

- **Transparency:** Project goals, budgets, and challenges are posted in a shared dashboard so everyone knows where things stand.

- **Generosity:** Team members freely share tools, templates, and tips with each other to save time and elevate the quality of everyone's work.

Forming Activity 4: Planning for Conflict and Failure

Let's talk about something many of us would rather avoid: conflict.

You might be thinking, *If we do all of these forming activities, won't that prevent conflict?*

Yes...and no.

At the risk of over-repetition, revisit Benjamin Franklin's famous line: "If you fail to plan, you are planning to fail."

Most people associate that quote with project timelines or business goals. But it applies just as well to team dynamics, especially in high-stakes collaboration.

The truth is: conflict will happen.

It's not a sign of failure. It's a sign that people care, that different perspectives are being surfaced, and that we're engaging in real work. But when conflict or failure catches us off guard, it can derail momentum, damage trust, and leave lasting wounds.

That's why we recommend planning for conflict *before* it happens. And we mean *literally* planning for it—out loud, together, with clear expectations and agreements.

We facilitate this as a team discussion using targeted prompts:

- What if someone doesn't deliver what they said they would?

- What if a teammate says something that upsets you?

- What if you disagree with a decision or direction, how will you raise it?

- What if someone's behavior starts to erode trust? What do we do?

- What happens when someone underperforms or drops the ball?

The goal isn't to predict every possible problem. It's to normalize the idea that things *will* go wrong, and to build a shared strategy for how you'll respond together.

Once you've named a few potential situations, ask the group: "What would we want to do if this happened?" and "How do we agree to respond?"

FAILURE ACTION	OUR AGREED TO REACTION
What if someone doesn't deliver what they said they would?	How do we agree to respond?
What if a teammate says something that upsets you?	How do we agree to respond?
What if you disagree with a decision or direction?	How do we agree to respond?
What if someone's behavior starts to erode trust?	How do we agree to respond?
What happens when someone underperforms or drops the ball?	How do we agree to respond?
Other...(continue on)	Other...(continue on)

You're not assigning blame or anticipating the worst. You're building a safety net.

And when something *does* go sideways (because it will), you can say: "Hey, remember how we agreed we'd bring it up when something like this happened? Well, it feels like we've hit one of those moments. Let's talk about it."

That kind of proactive, shared commitment doesn't just prevent drama. It builds maturity, accountability, and deeper trust. It tells your team: **we can handle the hard stuff together.**

FAILURE ACTION	OUR AGREED TO REACTION (EXAMPLE)
What if someone doesn't deliver what they said they would?	We will first check in with curiosity ("What got in the way?") and work together to reset expectations or adjust support. Patterns of missed commitments will be addressed directly.
What if a teammate says something that upsets you?	We will approach the person privately, share how the comment landed, and ask for clarity before assuming intent. If needed, we'll involve a neutral third party.
What if you disagree with a decision or direction?	We will voice concerns respectfully and provide reasoning. Maybe starting with "I am going to be brave/vulnerable and voice a disagreement/different perspective" to signal to everyone that we are enacting this agreed upon behavior. Once a final decision is made, we will align and move forward as a team.
What if someone's behavior starts to erode trust?	We will name the concern early, give specific examples, and discuss how to repair trust together rather than letting it fester.
What happens when someone underperforms or drops the ball?	We will first check in with curiosity ("What happened or got in the way?"). We will offer support, clarify expectations, and create an improvement plan. If the issue continues, we will escalate appropriately and with transparency.
Other...(continue on)	Other...(continue on)

Forming Activity 5: Build Your Space Makers

By this point, your team has done some important work: You've shared working styles, surfaced personal values, and created plans for how to navigate conflict and failure.

Now it's time to translate all that insight into something visible, usable, and grounding: **a set of group ground rules.**

We call this activity *Build Your Space Makers* because that's what these ground rules do. They create the psychological and relational space where great collaboration can happen.

To begin, facilitate a discussion that brings together everything you've surfaced so far:

- Working styles and preferences
- Shared values and what they look like in action
- Agreements about conflict and repair

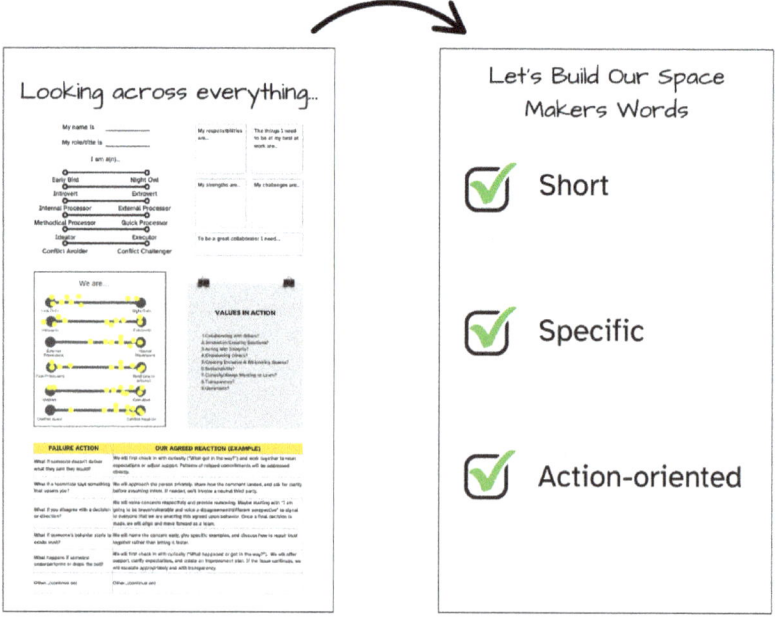

Then, ask the group: "Based on all of this, what do we need to remember every time we're together in order to collaborate well?"

What emerges becomes your list of *Space Makers*—the 5 to 7 norms or behaviors that everyone commits to. Keep them short, specific, and **action-oriented**. Examples might include:

- Assume positive intent
- One person speaks at a time
- No question is a bad question
- Listen to understand, not to respond
- Be brave and speak up
- Honor breaks and rest
- Capture the decisions we make

Once finalized, these ground rules aren't just a one-time output. They should be:

- **Visible** (in the room or on your digital board)
- **Referenced regularly** (especially at the start of meetings)
- **Living** (revisited and revised as needed)

We've seen teams transform simply by committing to this simple practice: **Re-grounding in their shared agreements, every time they come together.**

It's not about being rigid. It's about being intentional. Here are some space maker words we commonly use when we facilitate with groups:

SPACE MAKER WORDS

Safe Space

This is a safe space for sharing. Allow yourself and others to say the things that need to be and want to be said. We create this safe space by specifically saying that we practice confidentially; meaning that the details and stories that are shared stay in the room, but the learning, ideas, and next steps can go.

Be Vulnerable

Share openly and encourage ideas that can take a bit of courage! Be vulnerable with yourself and with others.

Listen, Don't Judge

Listen with the intent to understand not with the intent to judge. In action, this looks like not assuming but being curious; paraphrasing what you heard and asking clarifying questions when needed.

Assume positive intent

Assume positive intent means start with the mindset that everyone is trying their best with the tools that they have. If something isn't working, it may be that people just don't have the right tools, knowledge, or experience. And all of that can be fixed.

Stay Engaged

To the extent possible, try to close your devices/put your phone down, and try not to multitask. Use this time to engage with each other and be in the moment.

NO Abbreviations

Try not to use any abbreviations. Spell everything out so that everyone is on the same page and there is no confusion or misunderstandings.

Forming Activity 6: Name Your Team

This next step might sound lighthearted, and maybe even a little silly, but it's backed by serious psychology. Giving your team a **name** fosters a sense of identity, unity, and belonging. It's not about branding. It's about bonding.

When a team names itself, it creates a shared **"we."**

This name becomes a shorthand for your values, your vibe, and the commitments you've made to each other.

Here's how we guide this process:

1. **Draw from what you've already surfaced.**
   Invite the group to revisit words, themes, and insights that emerged from the previous activities, and especially your values, working styles, and ground rules.

2. **Mind Map it together.**
   On a whiteboard or digital board, gather all the resonant words and phrases. See what patterns emerge. Start playing with combinations. What name might represent this group's shared spirit or aspirations?

3. **Get creative and don't be afraid of weird.**
   The names that stick aren't always serious or polished. In fact, the quirky ones are often the most beloved.

   - A group of deep thinkers who love process? **The Strategic Sloths.**
   - A curious crew of late-night workers? **The Curious Owls.**
   - A team that values humor and challenge? **The Chaos Tamers.**

4. **Test the name.**
    Once a few options emerge, do a quick gut-check. What feels most "you"? What name brings a smile, a nod, a spark of recognition?

5. **Use it.**
    Start your emails with it. Refer to it in meetings. Let it become a part of how you show up together.

Because here's the truth: A name is more than a label. It's a reminder:

- Of who you are together.
- Of what you've committed to.
- Of the culture you're building on purpose.

Forming Activity 7: Craft a Team Charter/Mission

Once a team understands who they are and how they want to work together, the next step is defining **why** they're coming together in the first place.

That's where the **Team Charter** comes in.

This activity helps the group clearly articulate the purpose, goals, and shared vision of their collaboration. It anchors the team in a common direction, especially when things get messy or momentum dips. Even if your department or organization has an overarching charter, creating one that's specific to *this team, this project, and this moment* makes a world of difference.

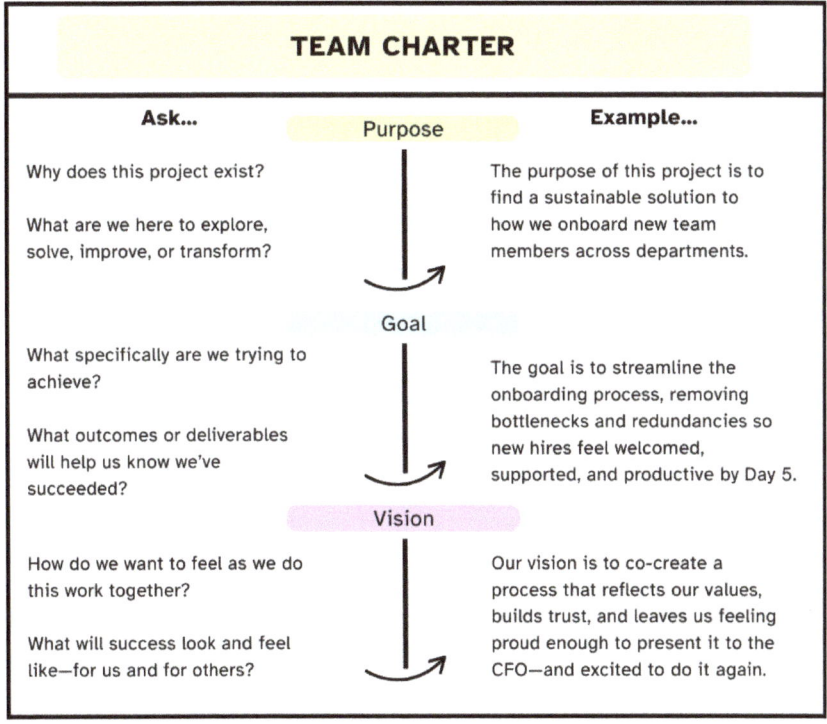

TEAM CHARTER

Ask...	Purpose	Example...
Why does this project exist? What are we here to explore, solve, improve, or transform?		The purpose of this project is to find a sustainable solution to how we onboard new team members across departments.

Goal

What specifically are we trying to achieve? What outcomes or deliverables will help us know we've succeeded?		The goal is to streamline the onboarding process, removing bottlenecks and redundancies so new hires feel welcomed, supported, and productive by Day 5.

Vision

How do we want to feel as we do this work together? What will success look and feel like—for us and for others?		Our vision is to co-create a process that reflects our values, builds trust, and leaves us feeling proud enough to present it to the CFO—and excited to do it again.

Here's how we guide the activity:

Start with a facilitated conversation around three key questions:

Purpose
- Why does this project/team/product/program exist? What are we here to explore, solve, improve, or transform?

  Example: The purpose of this project is to find a sustainable solution to how we onboard new team members across departments.

Goal
- What specifically are we trying to achieve? What outcomes or deliverables will help us know we've succeeded?

  Example: The goal is to streamline the onboarding process, removing bottlenecks and redundancies so that new hires feel welcomed, supported, and productive by Day 5.

Vision
- How do we want to feel as we do this work together? What will success look and feel like—for us and for others?

  Example: Our vision is to co-create a process that reflects our values, builds trust, and leaves us feeling proud enough to present it to the CFO—and excited to do it again.

Once the team has **co-written these three components**, document them in a visible, accessible way. This becomes your North Star. Refer back to it at key milestones. Use it as a gut-check when priorities shift or decisions feel tough.

Your team charter isn't just a statement—it's a signal. It says: We're not just here to do work. We're here to do it together, on purpose.

TEAM CHARTER

Purpose

The purpose of this project is to find a sustainable solution to how we onboard new team members across departments.

Goal

The goal is to streamline the onboarding process, removing bottlenecks and redundancies so that new hires feel welcomed, supported, and productive by Day 5.

Vision

Our vision is to co-create a process that reflects our values, builds trust, and leaves us feeling proud enough to present it to the CFO—and excited to do it again.

Forming Activity 8: Map Your Team's Collaboration Rhythm

Finally, no collaboration can thrive without clear communication—and not just *what* we communicate, but *how*, *when*, and *where*.

That's why we always close our team formation process with an intentional conversation about **collaboration rhythm**. It may not sound glamorous, but it's what keeps a team humming long after the kickoff.

We facilitate a discussion that covers three key areas:

Asynchronous Communication

This includes tools like email, shared docs, and other platforms that don't require everyone to be present at the same time.

Ask the group:

- Where will shared documents live?
- What channel will we use for official updates?
- How will we track meeting notes and decisions?

Example: A team may decide to create a shared Google Drive folder with sub-folders for agendas, notes, and deliverables. Official updates go to a dedicated group email, and all meeting notes are captured by an AI assistant and dropped into a "Meetings" folder.

Digital Synchronous Communication

This includes real-time tools like Slack, Teams, or text messaging. These platforms are great for quick clarifications, but they can also be overwhelming if not used with intention.

Ask the group:

- When is it appropriate to use these tools?
- What are our etiquette expectations?
- How do we make sure important decisions don't get lost in a thread?

Example: Slack is used for time-sensitive questions and decisions, with an agreement to be brief and direct. Anything requiring deeper thought or context gets bumped to email or the next meeting.

Meetings and Check-Ins

Now that working styles and preferences are on the table, you can design a rhythm that works for this group, and not just for the calendar.

Ask the group:

- What standing meetings do we need?
- How frequently should we check in?
- How do we build in time to pause, reflect, and adjust?

Example: The team agrees to meet biweekly on Tuesdays at 10am. A monthly "meta-meeting" is added to check progress, air concerns, and review the team's ground rules.

A predictable rhythm gives people peace of mind. Even if the rhythm needs to change (and it will), it's better to *start with a shared plan* than to leave everyone guessing. Because in collaboration, *communication isn't a byproduct—it's the backbone.*

Asynchronous Communication

Questions

- Where will shared documents live?
- What channel will we use for official updates?
- How will we track meeting notes and decisions?

Answers/Decisions

Example: Create a shared folder with subfolders for agendas, notes, and deliverables. Official updates go to a dedicated group email; meeting notes are captured by an AI assistant and dropped into a "Meetings" folder

Digital Synchronous Communication

Questions

- When is it appropriate to use these tools?
- What are our etiquette expectations?
- How do we make sure important decisions don't get lost in a thread?

Answers/Decisions

Example: Slack is used for time-sensitive questions and decisions, with an agreement to be brief and direct. Anything requiring deeper thought or context gets bumped to email or the next meeting.

Digital Synchronous Communication

Questions

- What standing meetings do we need?
- How frequently should we check in?
- How do we build in time to pause, reflect, and adjust?

Answers/Decisions

Example: Meet biweekly on Tuesdays at 10am. A monthly "meta-meeting" is added to check progress, air concerns, and review the team's ground rules.

Wrapping Up Chapter 7: Foundations That Last

When Tim reached out a year later, it wasn't because something was broken; it was because he wanted to build something right from the start. That's what this chapter has been all about.

Strong, sustainable collaboration isn't just about solving problems. It's about setting people up to *be* together well, through clarity, shared values, thoughtful structure, and human connection.

The tools we've shared may seem deceptively simple (such as the "Guide to Me" cards, timelines, team names, and rhythm check-ins), but don't underestimate their power. Each one helps build trust. Each one makes the invisible visible. And each one prepares a team not just to do the work, but to *do it well together.*

Whether you're launching a new collaboration or relaunching one that's drifted, these activities offer a starting point and a reminder:

- Collaboration is not something that just happens. It's something we design.

- A design is strongest when it honors the humans doing the work.

So go slow. Be deliberate. Set the stage.

And don't forget to name your team (We see you, Midnight Architects).

CHAPTER 8
Navigating Conflict in Collaboration

By now, you've seen the messy, beautiful, unpredictable nature of collaboration in action—from the early hesitations of Tim's team to their moments of breakthrough, miscommunication, and growth. If there's one truth we've learned in our work, it's this:

There is no collaboration without conflict.

Let's be honest: collaboration isn't all sticky notes and "we love this idea." Sometimes, it's eye rolls and awkward silences. Sometimes, it's people storming out. That's because collaboration involves humans...and humans, no matter how well-intentioned, are messy.

Every team eventually faces conflict. If you've been in any long-term collaborative project, you've probably seen it, felt it, or maybe even been the cause of it.

This chapter is about that moment when the collaboration gets hard. When someone gets hurt. When trust gets tested. When it feels easier to walk away than to work through it.

We call it *The Fire Test*. It's the phase where your team is forced to decide: Do we dissolve? Or do we evolve?

Here's the truth: there is no one-size-fits-all framework for conflict resolution. What we've found through years of work with leaders, educators, scientists, and nonprofit teams, is that the tools and principles we've already shared in this book *can be the repair tools.* They won't erase the tension, but they will help you walk through it together.

There is no collaboration without conflict.

What Makes Conflict So Hard?

Conflict isn't just about disagreement; it's about identity, trust, power, and emotion. It's what happens when the team moves from polite forming to real collaboration, and all the unspoken tension surfaces.

It doesn't always show up as yelling or slamming fists. In fact, more often it looks like this:

- Passive-aggressive comments ("Oh, *great idea.*")

- Withholding participation ("I'm just here so I don't get fired.")

- Challenging the facilitator's role or credibility

- Side conversations, sarcastic eye rolls, or texting under the table

- That heavy, sticky silence that signals something deeper than We're just thinking

From our experience, most conflict is not about the thing being discussed. It's usually about:

- **Miscommunication**: We thought we were talking about the same thing... we weren't

- **Lack of clarity**: Assumptions, unclear expectations, and "I thought you meant..." moments.

- **Fear**: Fear of being misunderstood, looking incompetent, or getting hurt

This is why we say: collaboration starts before the work begins. The more you can normalize clarity, vulnerability, and perspective-sharing early on, the easier it is to come back to each other when it gets difficult or even seemingly impossible.

Let's see how some of the principles you've learned come into play when things start to storm.

Collaboration   **Work**   **Success**

Conflict through the Principles of Collaboration

 *Make the Abstract Clear*

Conflict can escalate quickly when people are talking *around* each other. Or when they think they are talking about the same thing, but in reality, they have vastly different interpretations of the subject at hand.

Let's take a word almost everyone in an organization claims to value: **transparency**.

It's in our vision statements. Our team charters. Our ground rules.

Here's the irony: transparency is one of the most misunderstood—and most conflict-inducing—words in the workplace.

Ask a group if transparency is important, and nearly every hand goes up. But ask what it looks like in practice? You'll get wildly different answers. For one person, transparency means sharing *everything*: thoughts in progress, draft ideas, decision-making rationale, even the messy parts. For someone else, transparency means sharing *what's necessary*: the final decision and the reasoning behind it, but not every in-between step. To one person, over-communicating feels honest. To another, it feels chaotic or unfiltered.

Now imagine these two people on the same team, working on a high-stakes project. One keeps expecting more information and wondering, *Why are things being hidden?* The other thinks they're being transparent by sharing clear, concise updates. Tension builds. Trust frays. And all of it stems from assuming they meant the same thing by a single word.

This is why *making the abstract clear* matters so much in collaboration. It's not enough to say the word "transparency"—we have to define it, map it, and give it form.

When we name a value like transparency, we also need to ask:
- What does that look like in action? Get specific. Give examples.
- When is it helpful? When is it too much?
- What do we all agree it will mean and look like to us?
- How will we address it if we feel someone isn't transparent?

That's why Principle 1 is essential: get it out of your head and into the open. Visualize it. Define it. Draw it, name it, map it. Sticky notes aren't just for brainstorming—they are for conflict prevention and repair.

Until we do, we risk speaking the same language but living in completely different worlds.

 ### *Stop Assuming*

Assumptions are invisible…but they're loud.

They live in the silences between emails, in the quick glances across a meeting table, in the meanings we assign to someone else's words or actions. More often than not, our assumptions are wrong.

Stop and read that again. More often than not, our assumptions are wrong.

Which is why Principle 2—*Stop Assuming*—is essential, especially in moments of conflict.

One time, we worked with a cross-functional team where tension had quietly grown between two leads: Tracy, the strategist, and Don, the engineer. Tracy was frustrated because she felt Don kept rewording her ideas in meetings, and she felt undermined. Don, for his part, thought he was doing exactly what Tracy wanted. "We're just workshopping together," he said. "That's how we stress-test ideas, right?"

They weren't trying to offend each other. They were trying to collaborate—just from very different assumptions about what good collaboration looked like.

When we introduced a visual "About Me" board and had each team member share how they work, what they need from others, and what makes them shut down, the truth emerged. Tracy said she needed a moment of affirmation before receiving critique.

Don was stunned. "I had no idea."

That one small moment of shared clarity defused a month's worth of tension.

And assumptions don't just surface in live meetings. Here's a smaller but equally telling example:

You send an email to your team asking for feedback by Friday. Friday comes and goes. One teammate, Priya, doesn't reply. You start to spiral: *Is she annoyed with me? Checked out? Passive-aggressively refusing to help?*

But here's what really happened: Priya assumed your email was an FYI and that you'd follow up when the request became urgent. She wasn't ignoring you—she was interpreting your words through her own lens.

The antidote?

A simple message: "Hey Priya, I realize I might not have been clear when I requested feedback last week. Were you thinking feedback was optional, or that I'd ping you again later?"

Nine times out of ten, that kind of gentle curiosity dissolves the tension before it calcifies into resentment.

So much of what feels personal is actually structural. What seems like resistance is often misunderstanding. What looks like disengagement might just be someone playing by a different, unspoken rulebook.

Stop Assuming means surfacing these rulebooks. It means replacing your silent script with an honest check-in. It means remembering this: people aren't mind readers, even when we wish they were.

 *Just Say It*

There's a common misconception about honesty at work: saying what you really think will break things.

On the contrary, when Principle 1 (*Make the Abstract Clear*) and Principle 2 (*Stop Assuming*) are in place, Principle 3 (*Just Say It*) becomes the bridge between tension and transformation. It's not about being blunt or reckless—it's about voicing the thing that needs to be voiced, in a way that invites others in. Let's go back to Tim's team.

In their early sessions, we watched a dynamic play out in silence. Marcus (who was fast-talking and full of ideas), often interrupted or reshaped people's contributions before they were fully shared. Jessica, a thoughtful but quieter team member, stopped talking altogether. The air got tight, like everyone was holding back.

We cue-called it.

We said, "Marcus, we notice you're jumping in quickly, and your energy and enthusiasm are clearly driving the conversation. Jessica, we noticed you haven't said much today, is there anything you've been holding back?"

Then Tim stepped in, not to reprimand, but to recalibrate.

"Marcus, I know your brain moves fast and you're trying to help shape ideas in real-time. But I think we need to give people a little more space to finish their thoughts before we respond. Jessica, I felt like you were about to share something. Would you like to jump in?"

That moment changed the room. Not because someone was called out—but because someone was called in.

That's the heart of Principle 3: Saying what needs to be said, not as a weapon, but as an invitation.

It shows up in everyday moments too. Picture this:

You're in a project meeting, and your coworker Sam seems tense. They've been unusually quiet. You sense something is off, but you hesitate. *Maybe it's not my place. Maybe I'm imagining it. Maybe something is going on in Sam's personal life, and I shouldn't butt in.*

But part of *Just Say It* is trusting what you're sensing—especially if psychological safety has been built.

You say, "Hey, Sam, you've seemed a bit quieter today than usual. Anything on your mind or anything you want to weigh in on?"

Maybe they brush it off. Maybe they open up. Either way, you've opened the door.

Dostoyevsky said: "Much unhappiness has come into the world because of things left unsaid."

Conflict often festers in what's unsaid. We tiptoe around discomfort, hoping it'll go away. But silence doesn't solve...it stretches and lingers. On the other hand, when someone names what's happening in the room with care, it creates space for honesty and healing.

Of course, tone matters. Timing matters. But the message is simple:

"Saying it" kindly and clearly often keeps the group from breaking.

The more you model it, the more others will, too.

 ### *Slow Down to Speed Up*

When things get tense, our instinct is often to move faster. Fix it. Decide now. Wrap it up.

But collaboration isn't a race. It's a process. When conflict arises, slowing down often brings the clarity that speed can't.

Let's revisit a moment from a different client session.

> Two department leads, Jordan and Leah, were butting heads over a product rollout timeline. Their tones were sharp. Their postures, stiff. Each was convinced the other was being difficult, going so far as to mutter "jerk" under their breath.
>
> We paused the meeting.
>
> "Let's step back," we said. "Can we map the entire process, from start to finish, using sticky notes?"
>
> Everyone groaned a little. But they did it. Together, they built the full timeline: marketing efforts, testing, procurement, staff onboarding, etc.
>
> Halfway through, Jordan leaned back and said, "Oh. I thought you were trying to delay the launch. But you're just trying to make sure training is complete first."
>
> Leah replied, "Exactly. I wasn't trying to slow us down! I was trying to make sure we don't blow it."
>
> They weren't in conflict about the goal. They just hadn't seen the same picture.

That's the power of Principle 4 (*Slow Down to Speed Up*). It creates shared understanding by stepping back before pushing forward, particularly if we don't want to elbow people in the process.

Here's a smaller-scale example:

You're in a meeting where two team members disagree on how to distribute a survey. One wants to send it ASAP to meet a deadline. The other wants more input before it goes out.

Rather than debate it to death, you ask, "What do we need to better understand or consider before making this decision?"

This slows the conversation. Creates reflection. Reveals nuance. And often, surfaces hidden constraints or opportunities.

When you feel urgency pulling the group into friction or confusion, try asking:

- "What's the real problem we're trying to solve?"
- Or simply, "Can you help me understand why?"

We've seen this shift dynamics more times than we can count.

Slowing down doesn't mean doing less; it means doing what matters most, together. Slowing down makes the path forward clearer, faster, and stronger.

 ### *Walk Away with Something Actionable*

If there's one thing that can turn a small conflict into a long-term rift, it's inaction. Nothing deflates a team faster than working through a tough conversation, only to walk away with no clarity, no momentum, and no next steps.

Let's revisit a real moment from a workshop we facilitated. A cross-functional group had just spent the morning debating two radically different redesign concepts. Voices had raised. The energy was hot. By the time lunch rolled around, the group was split down the middle with no clear way to decide which concept to select for the afternoon.

Rather than force consensus or keep debating, we paused and asked:

- "What do we know right now?"
- "What don't we know?"
- "What could we do next that helps us learn more?"

That shift from resolving to exploring unlocked movement. Instead of choosing one concept over the other, they decided to prototype both and test them with users. That small, actionable step didn't solve the disagreement; it moved them forward and took the heat out of the room.

Here's another everyday example:

You're in a team meeting. A tough discussion about roles and responsibilities just wrapped. Tension lingers. Everyone's looking around, unsure what happens next.

Instead of letting the awkward silence stretch, you say:

- "What feels like a natural next step based on what we just discussed?"

- "Is there something small we could try this week to test a new way of working?"

When you create micro-movements, you give people purpose and a sense of agency. You also reduce the space where assumptions and resentment breed.

A few of our favorite tactics for this:

- **End each session with a quick round of "next right steps."** Keep it simple: what, who, by when, and how we'll know it's done.

- **Nominate an "Activator."** This person helps track progress, check in, and keep energy flowing between meetings.

- **Communicate even when there's no progress.**
  Transparency, even when things are slow, keeps conflict
  from growing in the silence.

In conflict, clarity is kindness. Even if you haven't resolved
everything, make sure the group leaves with direction. It reminds
people that momentum is possible and that their time and courage
mattered.

 *Plan to Pivot*

You planned the session. You built the agenda. You mapped the
steps toward the goal.

But then... something doesn't feel right.

This is where Principle 6 (*Plan to Pivot*) comes in.

Planning to Pivot isn't about having a perfect backup plan.
It's about being present enough to notice when the group needs
something different—and brave enough to follow that need. Let's
take you into one of our real sessions.

> We were facilitating a two-day workshop with a
> leadership team charged with creating a 3-year strategic plan.
> Day one was all about laying the foundation: identifying
> priorities, aligning on outcomes, surfacing shared
> aspirations. On paper, the agenda was solid.
>
> But one hour in, we could tell something was off.
>
> There was polite participation, sure...but underneath
> that, we noticed:
>
> - Passive-aggressive comments laced with sarcasm
> - Crossed arms, darting glances, slumped posture
> - People agreeing out loud while visibly disengaged

The energy was fractured. The group was saying yes, but their bodies were saying no.

Rather than forge ahead to the next activity, we called a break. While the group refueled with coffee and fruit, we huddled in the hallway and asked ourselves: "What's actually going on here? We can't go on to the next section and build that strategic plan unless we figure out what is going on and get them past it."

We decided to pivot.

When the group came back together, we said:

"Before we keep pushing forward on strategy, it feels like there might be some of what we call "pebbles in our collective shoes"—little (or not-so-little) things that might be making it hard to fully focus on building a strategic plan. So, we are going to pivot a bit and see if we can help with that."

We handed everyone sticky notes and asked them to list all the frustrations, blockers, and tensions they were carrying into the room. Anything that was distracting them, irritating them, or making this work feel harder than it needed to be, we wanted them to write down on the sticky notes.

What came out was revealing: *a lack of clarity around decision-making authority*. This issue wasn't on the agenda, but it cast a shadow over every discussion.

So, we scrapped the rest of the morning's plan and turned our focus to what had emerged. We facilitated a short DARCI (which is a roles and responsibilities matrix that helps the group identify who is a Decision Maker, who is Accountable, Responsible, Consulted, and Informed) activity to help clarify and build consensus on decision making authority. Only then did we return to the strategic plan.

Did we get as far into the plan that day as we originally hoped? No.

But did we unlock what was actually blocking the group's

ability to do the work? Absolutely.

That's the heart of *Plan to Pivot:* recognizing conflict or tension isn't an interruption. It's information.

Sometimes the most strategic thing you can do is stop planning strategy, and address what's keeping people from showing up fully.

The Power of Perspective

Much of this chapter has been about tools. But let's also talk about perspective, and how you can build your tolerance for tension over time.

One of our favorite resources is the book *Supercommunicators* by Charles Duhigg. He outlines that most conversations fall into one of three types:

- Practical conversations—focused on facts, outcomes, solutions
- Emotional conversations—driven by feelings, identity, values
- Social conversations—shaped by roles, belonging, power dynamics

Conflict often happens when two people are in different conversations, but don't know it.

A personal example:

You're talking with your spouse, trying to plan the logistics for your next family trip (flight options, budgets, dates, activities, etc.). Meanwhile, they're reminiscing: "Remember that sunset on the beach in Maui? That was magical."

You're in a **practical** conversation. They're having an

emotional one. Suddenly, you're frustrated because nothing is getting decided, and they're confused about why you're "rushing past the moment."

Neither of you is wrong. But you're not in the same conversation.

A professional example:

You're in a team meeting discussing how to fix a project bottleneck. You say, "Let's look at the workflow and update the process map."

Your colleague responds with, "I just feel like no one respects how much pressure we've been under. We've been bending over backward, and no one seems to care."

You're focused on **practical** problem-solving. They're surfacing **emotional** exhaustion.

Again, neither colleague is "wrong", they're just different conversations. That's why good collaborators, and good conflict navigators, listen for the type of conversation first. They ask themselves:

"Is this about solving a problem, expressing a feeling, or figuring out where we stand with each other?"

And if they're unsure? They name it out loud.

"Hey, I'm hearing this as a practical conversation about decisions. But it seems like there might be something emotional underneath, too. Am I missing something?"

This is a skill. Like any skill, it takes personal and social awareness and practice. Once you start tuning into what kind of conversation is actually happening, you'll be amazed how many near-misses you can avoid and how many tensions you can gently defuse.

See the Person. Not Just the Position

There's a saying coined by Brené Brown we come back to often: **"It's easier to hate from afar than from up close."**

So much conflict gets amplified, or even created, when people are distant from each other. Whether it's physically distant, emotionally distant, hierarchically distant, with distance we fill in the blanks with assumptions. We build stories about each other. And these stories are rarely generous.

That's why one of the simplest, most powerful things you can do in a conflict is to ***bring people together.*** Sit across from one another at a table, look each other in the eyes, and speak human-to-human. It sounds obvious, but we can't overstate how different it feels to connect face-to-face instead of through a Slack thread, email chain, or Zoom—especially in fast-moving or high-stakes work environments.

When we're actually in a room together, we pick up on tone, body language, micro-reactions. We share space. We *see* each other.

Once you've seen someone—once you've heard about the project they're juggling, the personal stress they're carrying, the reason they reacted the way they did—it's harder to reduce them to being "difficult," "annoying," or "the problem."

This is why we love to bring people into story-based activities when tension is high. Ask them to share something, anything, that reveals a piece of their humanity:

- Tell me about a time you failed and learned from it.
- Describe a moment when you felt really proud of your work.
- What is an ordinary moment in your life that brings you pure joy?

These are not magic questions. But they *build empathy*, fast. Once empathy is present, the dynamic begins to shift. People stop trying to win. They stop trying to see the other person as the villain. They start trying to understand.

Note: We know that there are many teams that are remote and primarily meet and connect on Zoom. And we know for these teams, the idea of "bringing people together" might be really hard. We want to acknowledge that and say, IF and WHEN you can, especially the start of a new initiative, project, or plan, explore bringing people together for a 2-3 day retreat and do this "pre" collaborative work together in the same room. That time together will be invaluable in the long run!

Improv: Conflict Without Consequence

If you tend to avoid conflict, here's a wildly helpful tip: try improv.

One of the reasons many of us avoid conflict is because it feels loaded. Personal. Permanent. The stakes are high, the feelings are real, and the fallout can feel like too much to manage. If you are the type of person that naturally avoids conflict versus taking it on full charge, the moment you begin to sense a bit of conflict, you shut down. How can you change that? That's where **improvisation** becomes an unexpected but powerful training ground.

Improv allows us to explore tension, disagreement, status, and perspective *without consequence because* we're playing. There's no real-world risk. No reputation on the line. Just possibility.

Inside that possibility, something extraordinary happens: we stop avoiding conflict...and start playing with it.

Try This: The Expert Panel Game

One of our favorite games to use in workshops (especially when working with folks who either shut down in conflict or cling tightly to their beliefs) is something we call "Expert Panel ." It's a deceptively simple structure with a deeply revealing impact.

Here's how it works:

1. **Round One: Be the Expert.** Ask participants to think of something they love, care about, or are deeply passionate about. It can be *anything*:

   - Why sourdough bread baking is a form of therapy
   - Why the Percy Jackson book series is criminally underrated
   - Why Dungeons & Dragons builds life skills
   - Why public education is one of the greatest social equalizers

2. Each person takes the stage (or spotlight) for one minute and speaks with conviction, enthusiasm, and genuine love for the topic. They're the expert! No notes. Just passion.

3. **Round Two: Flip It.** Now, take that same topic *and argue the complete opposite*.

   - Why baking bread is the most frustrating waste of time
   - Why *Percy Jackson* is just mythology fanfic gone rogue
   - Why D&D is nothing but dice, distractions, and delusions
   - Why public education fails students and private alternatives should be the norm

4. Again, one full minute. Same conviction. Same energy. No sarcasm allowed.

What happens next is magic: participants start to debate themselves. People laugh. They squirm. They discover.

They realize they can argue both sides...and that both sides contain truths. They feel, often viscerally, how multiple truths can live in tension. They discover that *conflict* doesn't always mean *combat*. Sometimes, addressing conflict means sitting with discomfort and listening to complexity.

Without even realizing it, they've practiced:

- Perspective-taking
- Tolerance for ambiguity
- Non-attachment to a single truth
- Playing inside tension, rather than avoiding it

Because here's what's often underneath conflict: *a desperate need to be right.* To make the world tidy. Black or white. Good or bad. Hero or villain. But the world isn't that simple, and collaboration with all its humanness certainly isn't that simple. Improv helps us stretch our minds, loosen our grip, and laugh a little while we practice letting go of absolutes. So, when someone says, "But both of those things could be true..." We say, *Exactly*!

That opposite view—the one so different from your own— exists. And now, you've confronted it. Held its tension. Sat with its discomfort. You've felt it in your body. This means, the next time you meet it in real life, you won't flinch.

You'll be ready.

How to Support a Team Through Conflict

Here's what we've found most helpful when guiding teams through the fire of conflict.

1. Normalize Conflict

Let the group know from day one: "Conflict is part of the process. It's not a sign of failure; rather, it's a sign that we're getting real." Set the expectation early that tension will emerge, and that you welcome it. Friction is where alignment gets forged.

2. Plan for Conflict

Remember the "Planning for Conflict and Failure" activity from Chapter 7? This is where it becomes gold. Revisit that plan. Remind the group what they said they'd do *when*, not *if*, tension arises. Let the group evolve their conflict norms as needed.

3. Surface Conflict Gently

Use your tools: cue-calling, reframing, and reflection. Here are a few lines we keep in our pocket:

- "It feels like there's some hesitation—what's behind it?"
- "I'm sensing there's something unspoken here. Would anyone like to name it?"
- "I noticed a shift in energy when that was said. Let's pause for a second—what's going on?"

You're not calling anyone out. You're calling *it* out, whatever "it" is. You're naming the tension without blame.

4. Return to the Ground Rules

When in doubt, return to what the group said mattered.

- "We agreed to assume positive intent."
- "We said we wanted to be brave, not just polite."
- "We promised to listen to understand."

These agreements aren't just meeting openers. They're guideposts.

5. Build the Muscle of Repair

Conflict is inevitable. What matters is whether the group has the language and courage for *repair*. Here are a few phrases we love:

- "Can we pause? I think that landed harder than intended."
- "That came out sharp. Let me try again."
- "I'm realizing I misunderstood—would you be open to a do-over?"

Practicing this kind of language doesn't just heal the moment. It builds a culture of humility, accountability, and care.

 *Final Truth: You Don't Have to Like Everyone*

Let's end with something no one really says out loud, but everyone needs to hear:

Even if you apply every principle in this book...

Even if you design the most thoughtful collaboration session...

Even if you name the tensions, slow down, reflect, and pivot...

Some people still won't click.

And that's okay.

Collaboration doesn't require friendship. It doesn't require shared hobbies or out-of-work socializing.

Sometimes, personalities clash.

Sometimes, communication styles grind.

Sometimes, you just don't like each other.

But here's the thing: collaboration isn't about liking, it's about *working well together anyway*.

It's about finding enough mutual respect, clarity, and structure to move forward without making things harder than they need to be.

If someone's not your cup of tea, you don't have to fake it. You just have to:

- Practice clarity
- Set good boundaries
- Use the tools
- Bring your best effort, even if the vibe isn't great

In our experience, even the most conflict-ridden pairings can find a way to function, and sometimes even surprise themselves when there's a shared purpose, a solid container, and just enough humanity to keep things from boiling over.

Sometimes, finding common ground as individuals is really challenging. However, something brought you to the collaboration, and if you're part of the same organization, something brought you both to that organization. So sometimes "the tie that binds" you together could be the shared mission of the organization and reminding yourself of that can help. You don't have to love everyone, but you *can* learn to work alongside them with integrity, care, and maybe even a touch of grace.

This is what good collaboration is all about.

A Call to Collaborate

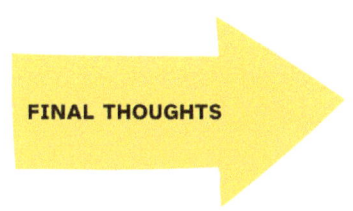

FINAL THOUGHTS

By now, you've seen it all: the awkward beginnings, the silence, the sparks, the tension, the breakthroughs. You've met Tim. You've watched a team fall apart, and then re-build something better.

You've walked through the six principles of collaboration. You've seen how structure becomes freedom, how vulnerability becomes strength, and how ordinary people—maybe even you— can hold the room, shape the moment, and help others move forward together.

Maybe now you're wondering: *Can I really do this? Can I lead collaboration that matters? Can I help people find their way to each other?*

Yes. You can.

Not because it's easy. It isn't.

Not because you'll always get it right. You won't.

But because this moment in history **needs you** to.

The world is complex, fractured, and moving fast.

Polarization is rising. Trust is eroding. Institutions are strained.

And the problems we face—things like climate, inequality, misinformation, global health—*cannot* be solved alone.

We need people who can lead across differences.

We need people who can hold discomfort without running from it.

We need people who can build bridges, especially when it feels impossible.

That's what high-stakes collaboration is. It's not soft. It's not fluffy. It's not "just another meeting."

It's world-building work. It's future-shaping work.
And now, you have the tools. The stories. The blueprint.

So use them.

Not just in the big moments, but in the daily ones: In meetings, in hallway chats, in group texts, in late-night decks, in early morning planning calls.

Every time you choose clarity over assumption, care over control, curiosity over judgment, you're not just collaborating You're showing what leadership looks like in the world we're in.

STAY CONNECTED

Resources

Support your team with additional resources, activity guides, book discussions, keynote booking requests, and much more!

CollaborationIllusion.com

ACKNOWLEDGMENTS

We wrote this book because collaboration is messy—and we learned that from all of *you*.

To the leaders, teams, board members, students, improv groups, design partners, and brave humans who let us into your world: thank you for the trust, the candor, and the real-life stories that shaped every chapter.

To our clients and partners across higher education, K-12 education, the health industry, private sector, non-profit sector, Fortune 500, and everyone in-between: thank you for giving us front-row seats to the challenges and breakthroughs that inspired this work.

To the people who read draft after draft, caught our blind spots, and reminded us what clarity really sounds like: this book is better because of you.

To our families, who endured our late-night writing marathons, endless conversations about Tim, and walls full of sticky notes: thank you for cheering us on and keeping us grounded. We couldn't have done it without your support and love.

REFERENCES

1   Tomasello, M., Carpenter, M., Call, J., Behne, T., & Moll, H. (2005). "Understanding and sharing intentions: The origins of cultural cognition." *Behavioral and Brain Sciences*, 28(5), 675–691. https://doi.org/10.1017/S0140525X05000129

2   Nuvolari, Alessandro. 2004. "Collective Invention during the British Industrial Revolution: The Case of the Cornish Pumping Engine." *Cambridge Journal of Economics* 28, no. 3 (May): 347–63. https://doi.org/10.1093/cje/28.3.347.

3   https://teamstage.io/project-management-statistics/

4   https://electroiq.com/stats/project-management-statistics/

5   https://www.mckinsey.com/capabilities/operations/our-insights/increasing-transparency-in-megaproject-execution

6   https://explodingtopics.com/blog/project-management-stats

7   Bibb Latané, Kipling Williams, and Stephen Harkins. "Many Hands Make Light the Work: The Causes and Consequences of Social Loafing." *Journal of Personality and Social Psychology*, vol. 37, no. 6, 1979, pp. 822-832.

8   Microsoft Work Trend Index: Annual Report – "Will AI Fix Work?" (2023).

9   Hailey Mensik, "The True Cost of Meetings, by the Numbers," WorkLife.News, April 25, 2024.

10 Roy F. Baumeister and Mark R. Leary, "The Need to Belong: Desire for Interpersonal Attachments as a Fundamental Human Motivation," *Psychological Bulletin* 117, no. 3 (May 1995): 497–529.

11 Evan W. Carr, Andrew Reece, Gabriella Rosen Kellerman and Alexi Robichaux. "The Value of Belonging at Work," *Harvard Business Review*, December 2019.

12 BetterUp Labs, The Connection Crisis: Why Community

Matters in the New World of Work. (2022).

13 Elise Keith, "The 16 Types of Business Meetings (and Why They Matter)," Lucid Meetings Blog.

14 López, Cary Jensine Sanden. "How Teams Navigate the Ebbs and Flows of Hope in Organizational Life." PhD diss., Arizona State University, 2023.

15 Amy C. Edmondson, "The Role of Psychological Safety: Maximizing Employee Input and Commitment," *Leader to Leader* 2019: 13–19.

16 Stephen M. R. Covey and Rebecca R. Merrill, *The Speed of Trust: The One Thing That Changes Everything* (New York: Free Press, October 2006), 125–43.

17 Patrick Lencioni, *The Five Dysfunctions of a Team: A Leadership Fable* (San Francisco, CA: Jossey-Bass, 2002).

18 James R. Detert and Amy C. Edmondson, "Implicit Voice Theories: Taken-for-Granted Rules of Self-Censorship at Work," *Academy of Management Journal* 54, no. 3 (June 2011): 461–88; Ruth Wageman, J. Richard Hackman, and Erin Lehman, "Team Diagnostic Survey: Development of an Instrument," *Journal of Applied Behavioral Science* 41, no. 4 (December 2005): 373–98).

19 Fred Luthans, Kyle W. Luthans, and Brett C. Luthans, "Positive Psychological Capital: Beyond Human and Social Capital," *Business Horizons* 47, no. 1 (January–February 2004): 45–50.

20 Carol S. Dweck, *Mindset: The New Psychology of Success* (New York: Random House, 2006); Martin E. P. Seligman, "The President's Address," *American Psychologist* 54, no. 8 (November 1999): 559–62.

21 Sigal G. Barsade, "The Ripple Effect: Emotional Contagion and Its Influence on Group Behavior," *Administrative Science Quarterly* 47, no. 4 (December 2002): 644–75; Barbara L. Fredrickson, "The Role of Positive Emotions in Positive Psychology: The Broaden-and-Build Theory of Positive Emotions," *American Psychologist* 56, no. 3 (March 2001): 218–26.

22 Charles R. Snyder, Cherise A. Harris, et al., "The Will and

the Ways: Development and Validation of an Individual-Differences Measure of Hope," *Journal of Personality and Social Psychology* **60**, no. 4 (April 1991): 570–85.

23 López, Cary Jensine Sanden. "How Teams Navigate the Ebbs and Flows of Hope in Organizational Life." PhD diss., Arizona State University, 2023.

24 Patrice M. Buzzanell, "Resilience: Talking, Resisting, and Imagining New Normalcies Into Being," *Journal of Communication* 60, no. 1 (2010): 1–14.

25 López, Cary Jensine Sanden. "How Teams Navigate the Ebbs and Flows of Hope in Organizational Life." PhD diss., Arizona State University, 2023..

26 Amy C. Edmondson, "Psychological Safety and Learning Behavior in Work Teams," *Administrative Science Quarterly* 44, no. 2 (December 1999): 350–83.

27 Ronald S. Burt, *Brokerage and Closure: An Introduction to Social Capital* (Oxford: Oxford University Press, 2005); Mark S. Granovetter, "The Strength of Weak Ties," *American Journal of Sociology* 78, no. 6 (May 1973): 1360–80.

28 John P. Meyer and Natalie J. Allen, *Commitment in the Workplace: Theory, Research, and Application* (Thousand Oaks, CA: Sage Publications, 1997).

29 William A. Kahn, "Psychological Conditions of Personal Engagement and Disengagement at Work," *Academy of Management Journal* 33, no. 4 (December 1990): 692–724.

30 Gallup, Inc., *State of the Global Workplace: Understanding Employees, Informing Leaders* (Washington, D.C.: Gallup, June 2024).

31 Alan M. Saks, "Antecedents and Consequences of Employee Engagement," *Journal of Managerial Psychology* 21, no. 7 (2006): 600–19.

32 Rosaline S. Barbour, Doing Focus Groups (London: SAGE Publications, 2001)

33 Lu Hong and Scott E. Page, "Groups of Diverse Problem Solvers Can Outperform Groups of High-Ability Problem Solvers,"

Proceedings of the National Academy of Sciences of the United States of America 101, no. 46 (November 2004): 16385–89

34   López, Cary Jensine Sanden. "How Teams Navigate the Ebbs and Flows of Hope in Organizational Life." PhD diss., Arizona State University, 2023.

35   Teresa M. Amabile and Steven J. Kramer, "The Power of Small Wins," Harvard Business Review 89, no. 5 (May 2011)

36   Dan W. Grupe and Jack B. Nitschke, "Uncertainty and Anticipation in Anxiety: An Integrated Neurobiological and Psychological Perspective," Nature Reviews Neuroscience 14, no. 7 (July 2013): 488–501, doi:10.1038/nrn3524.

37   Bruce T. Montgomery and Gail Montgomery, The Improv Mindset: Change Your Brain. Change Your Business. (self-published as ExperienceYes, 2020)

38   Vicki Webster, Paula Brough, and Kathleen Daly, "Fight, Flight or Freeze: Common Responses for Follower Coping with Toxic Leadership," Stress and Health 32, no. 4 (2016): 346–354, https://doi.org/10.1002/smi.2626.

DISCLAIMER

Some images, illustrations, and visual elements in this book were created using licensed pro-level assets from Canva. Cover art and all design by the authors.

This text is set in Montserrat + Atkinson + Source Serif Pro for cohesive, readable, accessibility-forward engagement. Atkinson Hyperlegible is a typeface designed by Braille Institute specifically to maximize readability, especially for people with low vision or visual impairments.

The characters, scenarios, and stories in this book are inspired by real-world experiences and interactions. However, names, identifying details, timelines, and narrative elements have been altered or combined to protect the privacy and confidentiality of the individuals and organizations involved. Any resemblance to actual persons, living or dead, or actual events is coincidental and unintentional.

This book contains links to third-party websites provided for informational purposes only. The authors and publisher are not affiliated with and do not endorse or control these external sites or their content.

Web addresses and content may change or become inactive after publication. The authors and publisher are not responsible for the availability of linked sites or for any content, products, or services they provide. Users access external websites at their own risk.

All web addresses were accurate at time of publication. If you encounter a broken link, please search for the organization or resource by name.

ABOUT THE AUTHORS

Anca Castillo is a human-centered designer, strategic storyteller, and collaboration consultant known for bringing improv, visual thinking, and facilitation to leaders who want to communicate with clarity and build forward-thinking strategies together. As Co-Founder and Co-CEO of Design Convo, a consulting company focused on designing and facilitating conversations for impact, she helps organizations navigate complexity, align diverse stakeholders, and shape futures they believe in. Born and raised in Romania, she brings a global perspective to her work and her belief in the power of people coming together. Her background spans strategic planning, leadership development, futures thinking, and process design—expertise she uses to help teams think better together, build trust faster, and move ideas into action. She lives in Chandler, Arizona, with her family.

Cary Lopez, PhD is Co-Founder and Co-CEO of Design Convo, where she designs and facilitates workshops, trainings, and events while helping executives and leaders with strategic planning and organizational change. With over twenty years of experience leading strategic initiatives and transforming workplace culture, she brings a unique blend of credentials: certified public accountant (CPA), project management professional (PMP), and one of the first 500 certified change management professionals (CCMP) in the world. She holds master's and doctoral degrees in communication from Arizona State University—a combination she calls being a "pracademic," bridging the worlds of research and work. Her career spans for-profit and non-profit sectors, higher education, and computer software. Cary is also a founding board member of the Association of Change Management Professionals (ACMP) Arizona chapter, where she advocates for the professional development and recognition of change practitioners. She lives in Phoenix, Arizona with her family.

ABOUT THE PUBLISHER

Curious People Press is an independent, women-owned and operated publishing house based in Phoenix, Arizona. We exist for authors, artists, and advocates who care about the world and its inhabitants—and for readers who share that commitment.

Founded on the belief that curiosity opens doors and stories build bridges, we seek out work that challenges assumptions, deepens understanding, and moves people to action. Every title in our catalog reflects our dedication to amplifying voices that make a difference.

EDITORIAL BOARD

CURIOUS PEOPLE PRESS

Learn more at CuriousPeoplePress.com

www.ingramcontent.com/pod-product-compliance
Lightning Source LLC
Chambersburg PA
CBHW051616120626
46551CB00014B/1813